CREDITS

Recorded, Mixed & Mastered by Kristen Kreft and Mayalou Banatwala
Photography by Angie Lipscomb
Artist Renderings by Dylan Speeg
Cover Art, Layout Design & Graphics by Jeni Jenkins, Renegade Babe Studio
Bio Photo by Emily Maxwell
Published by Praus Press
Proofreading by Diane Lee Ross

Praus Press
306 Greenup St., Covington, KY, 41011

Copyright 2019 by Kristen Kreft and Mayalou Banatwala
All Rights Reserved

ISBN-13: 978-1-947934-03-0

THIS BOOK IS DEDICATED IN LOVING MEMORY TO OUR DEAR FRIEND ANGELA "HARV" HARVEY.

TABLE OF CONTENTS

FOREWORD 6

INTRODUCTION 8

ARTISTS & COCKTAILS 10-107

    JAMES BROWN 10
        COCKTAIL: POPCORN 13

    PATTI PAGE 14
        COCKTAIL: HUSH HUSH BOOGIE LOVE 15

    RUSTY YORK 16
        COCKTAIL: SUGAREE 17

    INK SPOTS 18
        COCKTAIL: WORLD'S ON FIRE 21

    BIG MAYBELLE 22
        COCKTAIL: MAYBELLE'S BLUES 23

    MEMPHIS SLIM 24
        COCKTAIL: HEY SLIM! 27

    LEMON PIPERS 28
        COCKTAIL: GREEN TAMBOURINE 31

    CATHY CARR 32
        COCKTAIL: IVORY TOWER 33

    OHIO PLAYERS 34
        COCKTAIL: JIVE TURKEY 37

RALPH STANLEY 38
    COCKTAIL: PRETTY POLLY 41

THE JUBALAIRES 42
    COCKTAIL: CHERRIES JUBALAIRES 43

ROSEMARY CLOONEY 44
    COCKTAIL: THE SWAY 47

BOBBY BARE 48
    COCKTAIL: TEQUILA SHEILA 49

MIDNIGHT STAR 50
    COCKTAIL: WET MY WHISTLE 53

JIMMY DORSEY 54
    COCKTAIL: AMAPOLA 55

HANK WILLIAMS 56
    COCKTAIL: HANKELADA 59

SKEETER DAVIS 60
    COCKTAIL: A MANHATTAN FOR THE END OF THE WORLD 63

MOUSE AND THE TRAPS 64
    COCKTAIL: MAID OF SUGAR MAID OF SPICE 65

BOBBY BYRD 66
    COCKTAIL: BABY BABY BABY 67

SPARKLE MOORE 68
    COCKTAIL: ROCK-A-BOP 71

BOOTSY COLLINS 72
   COCKTAIL: THE BOOTZILLA COLLINS 75

THE CASINOS 76
   COCKTAIL: THE CLASSIC CASINO COCKTAIL 77

VICKI ANDERSON 78
   COCKTAIL: SUPER GOOD 81

LONNIE MACK 82
   COCKTAIL: CINCINNATI JAIL OLD FASHIONED 85

THE DEELE 86
   COCKTAIL: BODY TALK 87

ISLEY BROTHERS 88
   COCKTAIL: THE CLASSIC BETWEEN THE SHEETS 91

KENNY SMITH 92
   COCKTAIL: FOXXXFIRE 93

NINA SIMONE 94
   COCKTAIL: REAL REAL 99

H-BOMB 100
   COCKTAIL: THE H-BOMB 101

HANK BALLARD 102
   COCKTAIL: THE TWIST 105

HARV 106
   COCKTAIL: THE HARVINATION 107

QUICK GUIDELINES 108
BREWS AND BOOZE 110
AUTHOR BIOGRAPHIES 112
ABOUT ROCKTAILS 113

FOREWORD

Giants rock among us. That's right. Legends and luminaries, some unsung, are all around us. Some are iconic in Europe, Asia, and Africa, while unnoticed locally.

But things are changing. People are waking up in the Cincinnati region. We are realizing invaluable contributions from these living treasures and through their music made in our backyards and on our front porches... even recorded in some unique buildings still standing. Have you seen The Three Kings of Otis Williams, Philip Paul and Bootsy Collins leading the charge in reviving King Records on Brewster in Evanston and at Herzog downtown? Take a look. Our revival is led by the real people. No need to fake it. We have what's authentic.

You can literally pretend you are Bob Dylan and find your own Woody Guthrie - someone who has somehow become neglected - and celebrate her or his music together. You can treat them like the queens and kings they are. You can do it. You can play their music to them. You can even make new music with them. You can do it in the footsteps of some of your mutual music heroes – even the ones who transitioned into full time spirits. For those giants who have passed on, so many of their family and friends remain. Talk to them. Allow inspiration to flow and find yourself creating new art in appreciation. Make it an event. Offer it up.

The legacy of our region's music and music-makers is ours here and now – if we want it. If you choose it. How old is rock 'n' roll? What about how young it is? What is rock 'n' roll? Isn't it a bunch of music styles coming together to create a new music? How do you choose to look at the facts? Will you arrange them and respect their essence to create a new narrative while steeped in traditions? Do you hear the music of yesteryear as present in songs yet to be sung? In comparison to musical genres hundreds, even thousands of years old, rock 'n' roll might be a toddler in its lifespan. Do you think it's all been done already or do you see the future in the moment at hand? Do you need to be a musician to participate? I don't think so. At all. This is communal and we can all have roles.

Seems to me, Kristen Kreft and Mayalou Banatwala are addressing many of these points and questions in this unique book. They are musicians, yes. But they are also authors and mixologists engaging in something new and different that could sweep across this nation. They have created an experience, not just a book, that can take you on a journey, filled with concoctions to drink, hear, taste, see and feel. It's more 3-D, like a Chaucer song. It doesn't surprise me at all. Both Maya and Kristen are no strangers to this kind of work. You typically can't get there until you pay some dues. They have definitely been building to this point and I only have a snapshot into that progress.

Marvin Hawkins, local musician and Cincinnati music historian, first introduced me to Kristen Kreft at a CityBeat Cincinnati Entertainment Awards show where she performed with Kenny Smith as a background vocalist in his one time backing band, Pearlene. Shake It Records had just re-issued Kenny Smith material and it was all tied to the Contemporary Arts Center's exhibit featuring Smith among other Cincinnati legends orbiting Soul, R&B and Funk from the last incarnation of life at "King Records" at 1540 Brewster. This was a musical collaboration with Darren and Jim Blasé, Dan McCabe and Chris Burgan to name a few. A few years later at the Historic Herzog studio space, I talked with Kristen and her father Paul Kreft about saving King Records and about their own legacy with Fraternity Records. (Paul worked at Counterpart and I think Kristen might have been on the last Fraternity releases from the Shad O'Shea era of Harry Carlson created Fraternity Records.)

Dave Cupp first introduced me to Mayalou Banatwala when she brought her ukulele to Herzog to rehearse with Train Kept A-Rollin Guitar Army Generals comprised of Scotty Wood, Edwin Vardiman, and Neil Sharrow as they prepared to take over Fountain Square on the 60th anniversary of the original jump blues recording of Tiny Bradshaw's "Train Kept A-Rolling" on Syd Nathan's King Records. We gathered with Mr. Bradshaw's family and kicked off the event with the beat of Bradshaw's drummer Mr. Philip Paul.

At a Herzog Music Kids Jam, one featuring Hanna Rae Mathey and a live band puppet show, Kristen shared with me her vision with Maya for a book on cocktails and Cincinnati music greats, to be paired with events paying homage to such history. It's a real joy to see all this come together. And to see how they involved so many others. Before this publication, Dylan Speeg was publishing on his Facebook thread amazing drawings of all these musicians with local ties. Those also caught my attention, and eventually led to me having the honor of writing this foreword.

So, anyway, much cheers to Kristen and Maya. Enjoy these Rocktails which bring fresh ways to engage in the rich and diverse music of our area. Respects to all works like this keeping time out of mind and the authentic in the present, while paying respects to our elders and traditions.

ELLIOTT RUTHER

[Songwriter of "Hand Me Down My Walkin' Cane Blues (Revisionist)" and "Rock-N-Roll Conceived (in Cincinnati)"; co-founder of modern Herzog era and Cincinnati USA Music Heritage Foundation; Mayor Cranley appointed Music Ambassador and King Records Steering Group]

INTRODUCTION

This is a collection of musical artists with a Cincinnati connection, and a cocktail that has been carefully curated in each of their honor. Some artists are well known, iconic even, with which the connection to the city may be clear and already defined. Some are more obscure and perhaps hidden under the sleeves of dusty records in the shadows of your local record store. Hopefully, you will find some surprises along the way, as we did during our research.

Upon digging into the trenches of Cincinnati's rich musical past, it has become apparent that the music business is and always will be a little twisted and riddled with oral tradition passed down from generation to generation. There are always at least two sides to a story. In our account the relationship between artist and label is one that sends almost every aspiring musician into a tornado of licensing and publishing, versus the creative freedom of the artist. We say cheers to those who learned how to ride the wave of popular music! Whether it be by standing their ground and holding true to their art 100%, or those who found a way to wind their funk into the very breath of the tracks put forth on the label.

In this book, we strive to find the soul of the artist, combine it with some factual history, and amp up traditional cocktails with our Rocktails' spin. Each ingredient in each drink is handpicked and intentional, uniquely portraying our interpretation of the musical artist with the utmost love and dignity. We hope that you enjoy reading the brief histories that we have provided, with the soundtrack of Cincinnati musical history wafting through the air, sipping reverently on the paired Rocktails we have so lovingly created for you.

Salud!

Kristen Kreft & Mayalou Banatwala

JAMES BROWN

MAY 3, 1933 TO DECEMBER 25, 2006

"THE HARDEST WORKING MAN IN SHOW BUSINESS."

The Godfather of Soul was born in a one room shack in the woods of Barnwell, South Carolina, near the Georgia state line, in 1933. When he was 4 years old, he was sent to live with his Aunt Honey, who was the madam of a brothel in Augusta, Georgia.

James was dismissed from school in the 6th grade for wearing "insufficient clothing" and thus began working as a child, wearing clothes made of burlap sacks, shining shoes, picking cotton and dancing in the streets.

While at his aunt's brothel, he learned to play the piano, guitar and harmonica and enjoyed entertaining the WWII troops who traveled near his home at the time.

As a teenager, James also had a brief career as a boxer, but by 16 was sent to prison for robbery. While in prison, JB formed a gospel singing group with some fellow cell mates and earned the nickname of "Music Box."

After a baseball game in the detention center outside of the prison, Brown met Bobby Byrd who had been playing on the opposing team, and had heard of this "Music Box" who could really sing. Byrd claimed his family was instrumental in getting James Brown released early from prison, which led to Brown promising the Court that he would dedicate his life to singing for the Lord. Brown joined Byrd's Gospel Group which eventually became the Flames, and in true JB fashion, Brown ended up being the front man of the Famous Flames. Thus, the "Hardest Working Man in Show Business" title was not just born, but wholeheartedly earned.

James was not just an entertainer, he also believed he should use his fame to focus on social issues, such as the importance of education and the power of being Black and proud, writing and recording the songs, "Don't Be a Dropout" and "Say it Loud, I'm Black and I'm Proud."

James was a tough band leader. By demanding perfection from his players, he helped bring several musician's careers to fruition, combining the rhythms of New Orleans, bass lines of the Blues, signature percussive electric guitar riffs, along with the vocal stylings of what helped to inspire the Hip Hop sound and the birth of Funk music.

HITS

"PLEASE PLEASE ME"

"SEX MACHINE"

"GET ON UP"   "I FEEL GOOD"

"SAY IT LOUD, I'M BLACK AND I'M PROUD"

"POPCORN"   "PAPA'S GOT A BRAND NEW BAG"

"HOT PANTS"   "I GOT THE FEELING"   "COLD SWEAT"

12 ROCKTAILS: AN AMPED UP SPIN ON MIXOLOGY

POPCORN

1½ oz Copper and Kings American Craft Brandy
   (or make it Funky with 2½ oz)
1 oz Caramel Popcorn Simple Syrup
½ oz Lemon Juice
½ oz Dolin Dry Vermouth
2 Dashes of Angostura Bitters
Sparkling Wine
Lemon Peel

✱✱✱ Combine brandy, simple syrup, vermouth, lemon juice and bitters in a mixing glass. Fill with ice. With a mixing tin, proudly shake yer money maker and strain into a rocks glass stacked with rocks. Top with sparkling wine and garnish with a couple lemon peels until it feels good. Serve with popcorn on the side for maximum *soul power*.

CINCINNATI CONNECTION

The "hardest working man in show business" recorded at King Records in Cincinnati, Ohio. His most famous record was released on King Records even though the label was adamantly against it, because it was to be live and debut new songs that were not approved yet by the label. James Brown's *Live at The Apollo* album is as iconic as the man himself. JB not only recorded at King but created his empire at King cultivating the careers of countless musicians.

"Thank you and thank you very kindly. It's indeed a great pleasure to present to you at this particular time, nationally and internationally known as the Hardest-Working Man in Show Business, the man who sings I'll Go Crazy! Try Me! You've Got the Power! Think! If You Want Me! I Don't Mind! Bewildered! Million-Dollar Seller, Lost Someone! The very latest release, Night Train! Let's everybody shout and shimmy! Mr. Dynamite, the amazing Mr. Please Please himself, the star of the show, James Brown and the Famous Flames!" - As quoted at the beginning of *"Live at the Apollo."*

PATTI PAGE

"THE SINGIN' RAGE, MISS PATTI PAGE."

NOVEMBER 8, 1927 TO JANUARY 1, 2013

Clara Ann Fowler was born into a large family with a very humble upbringing in Oklahoma; the towns of Muskogee and Claremore both claim to be her birthplace. Despite her meager means, she was able to graduate from high school in 1945, and by age 18, Patti was performing regularly on KTUL, a Tulsa Radio station. The program during which she was featured was sponsored by the Page Milk Company. On air, they addressed the young singer as Patti Page - she kept the nickname as her stage name.

Patti recorded her first single "Confess" on Mercury as the label's first female recording artist. This happened to be during an industry strike, leaving no background singers available to lay down tracks on the tune. Page, the Mercury label, and engineer Bill Putnam, decided to try their hand with a new recording technology and overdubbed Patti's harmony vocals, making Patti the first pop artist to harmonize with her own vocals on a recording, which also led to vocal credits as the "Patti Page Quartet." "Confess" became a top 15 hit on Billboard Magazine with the #12 spot on the Top Seller's chart. This was only the first of many hits Patti Page recorded.

Patti Page's second #1 hit (and all-time best seller) was "Tennessee Waltz." She was not the first artist to record or perform the song, but her version made history, camping out as #1 for 13 weeks in 1950-1951, selling seven million copies in the 1950s alone.

Ms. Page was one of the few Pop artists to remain on the charts during the rise of Rock 'n' Roll, and along with her continued success, she cultivated a relationship with live television programming, Broadway recordings and the silver screen gaining featured spots on all of the relevant live television shows of the era. Patti recorded the title track of the Bette Davis film *Hush Hush Sweet Charlotte* and was the first artist to record "The Sound of Music," which was released the same day the famed show opened on Broadway.

Patti Page was a crossover pioneer, and a queen of "firsts" with hits on the Pop, R&B and Country charts ("Tennessee Waltz" claimed #1 spots on all three charts concurrently). She dominated airwaves through the 1950s and 1960s, resulting in over 100 albums, 160 singles, 84 Top 40 Billboard Hits, and a Grammy. Patti Page remained a hardworking show woman performing and touring well into her 70s. Although she has passed, you may read her memoir *This is My Song* and hear Patti's story in her own words.

HITS "CONFESS" "WITH MY EYES WIDE OPEN, I'M DREAMING" "STEAM HEAT" "ALL MY LOVE (BOLERO)" "DETOUR" "TENNESSEE WALTZ" "HUSH HUSH SWEET CHARLOTTE" "I WENT TO YOUR WEDDING" "OLD CAPE COD" "HOW MUCH IS THAT DOGGY IN THE WINDOW" "THE SOUND OF MUSIC" "BOOGIE WOOGIE SANTA CLAUS" "I DON'T CARE IF THE SUN DON'T SHINE"

Hush Hush Boogie Love

1 oz Mead
1 oz White Grape Juice
¾ oz Averna
½ oz Apricot Syrup
Berries
Grapes
Mint

✱✱✱ Combine all ingredients in your drinking glass. Give a quick but loving stir, then with your eyes wide open, dreamily add in ice until the glass is full, continuing to stir. Top your cocktail with a pile of grapes, berries, and mint. *We must confess, this drink is just right for a steamy day in the summer sun.*

Cincinnati Connection

In June of 1951, Patti Page graced the Queen City by recording a handful of tunes with a country twinge at the Herzog Recording Studio. A few of the songs recorded you may find familiar are: "Tumbling Tumbleweeds," "I Want to Be a Cowboy's Sweetheart," "Detour," and "San Antonio Rose."

The Herzog Studio has been reopened and is a museum of recording history. You may visit it at 811 Race Street in Cincinnati, Ohio. Patti Page also performed with the Cincinnati Symphony Orchestra in 1997, which has been documented on video.

RUSTY YORK

> "...he could have told people that he could play any tune in any style. But he never bragged about it. ... He just did it."
> – LINDA YORK

MAY 24, 1935 TO JANUARY 26, 2014

Charles Edward York was born in 1935, in Harlan County, Kentucky. He and his family moved to the Cincinnati downtown hub, Over-The-Rhine, when he was 17. His sister gave him a second-hand guitar that happened to have the name "Rusty" scrawled onto its body. As he made his rounds in the Cincinnati club circuit playing Bluegrass with his gifted guitar, he became known simply as, "Rusty York."

Rusty soon desired to stir things up a bit musically and moved forward into a new sound delving into Rock 'n' Roll and Rockabilly. Rusty recorded a version of Buddy Holly's "Peggy Sue" on King records, which led him to join forces with Bonnie Lou of *Midwestern Hayride* for another Rockabilly project. Rusty's big hit was "Sugaree," which was in fact a Marty Robbins cover that Rusty recorded in 1959 at Cincinnati's legendary King Records studio. "Sugaree" quickly went "gold" charting #77 on the Billboard Music Chart. During "Sugaree's" success, Rusty and his band went on tour with Dick Clark's American Bandstand acts, and opened for Frankie Avalon and Annette Funicello at the Hollywood Bowl, becoming the first Rock 'n' Roll band to play the Bowl.

In 1964, Rusty went on tour with Bobby Bare as his band leader during Bare's climb to fame in the country music business. After touring around the country and performing in Las Vegas, Rusty began to focus more on his very own recording studio (a converted garage) in a Cincinnati suburb north of town. Jewel records was alive and pumping out records all the way into the early 2000's, where acts such as The Grateful Dead, Lonnie Mack, Ralph Stanley, and Cincinnati Bengals' Mike Reid spent time in the studio recording and creating music. "Sugaree's" success and staying power earned him a spot in the Rockabilly Hall of Fame in 1998.

HITS

"SUGAREE"

"TREMBLIN"

"RED ROOSTER"

"GOODNIGHT CINCINNATI, GOOD MORNING TENNESSEE"

16 ROCKTAILS: AN AMPED UP SPIN ON MIXOLOGY

SUGAREE

2 oz *New Riff Bourbon*
½ oz *Allspice Dram*
½ oz *Vanilla Syrup*
Madtree Rubus Cacao
Grated Nutmeg
Pumpkin Seeds
Dried Lemon Float

✱✱✱ Combine bourbon, Allspice Dram, and vanilla syrup in a mixing glass. Shake it, Sugaree, and strain into a stemless glass. Top with hearty frothy beer and sprinkle grated nutmeg. Float your seeds atop a dried lemon wheel and you've got yourself some *Rockabilly gold*.

CINCINNATI CONNECTION

Rusty is a Cincinnati legend who actually lived and resided in Cincinnati throughout most of his life. His career began in Over-the-Rhine and his love and knowledge of music spilled over into his Jewel Recording Studio located in the Cincinnati neighborhood of Mount Healthy. He recorded on King, Jewel, and Fraternity labels.

THE INK SPOTS

"DID YOU EVER SEE A DREAM WALKING?"

YEARS MOST ACTIVE 1934 TO 1954

The Ink Spots had a giant rotating cast of characters as there have been literally hundreds of musicians claiming the role of an Ink Spot. The official group started as a three-piece musical comedy team under the name "King, Jack, and Jester." A fourth member was added in 1934 and they became The 4 Ink Spots.

In 1934, The 4 Ink Spots lit up the Apollo stage with a performance so grand that the audience was left with dropped jaws from their groundbreaking sound. The group's signature style was all about the vocals and impeccable harmony, accompanied by stringed instruments, including a cello which was slapped and percussed as though it were an upright bass. They invented their method of Top and Bottom singing where the top tenor would sing melodies while the bottom bass would trade the chorus by reciting the lyrics in a spoken word rather than singing them.

In 1936, Billy Kenny replaced Jerry Daniels and the group finally landed on their title of The Ink Spots. Billy has been credited for leading the group to fame with his soaring tenor tones, further punctuating their patented Top and Bottom singing. The Ink Spots were integral in bringing the Doo-Wop sound of the 50's into the mainstream, not to mention popping up in more modern media, such as the opening to a Megadeth song, Martin Scorsese's films The Aviator and Raging Bull, as well as a cameo in an episode of The Simpsons. The Ink Spots were inducted into the Rock & Roll Hall of Fame in 1989 and the Vocal Group Hall of Fame in 1999.

HITS

"I DON'T WANT TO SET THE WORLD ON FIRE"

"DON'T GET AROUND MUCH ANYMORE"

"IF I DIDN'T CARE"

"I'M MAKING BELIEVE"

"INTO EACH LIFE SOME RAIN MUST FALL"

"ADDRESS UNKNOWN"

"I'M BEGINNING TO SEE THE LIGHT"

"JAVA JIVE"

WORLD'S ON FIRE

2 oz Rum (light or spiced)
1 oz Bailey's
1 oz Chai Tea
Bacardi 151
Tapioca Pearls
Cinnamon Stick

*** Combine rum, Bailey's, and tea in a mixing glass. Fill with ice. Shake it like the world depends on it. Coat martini glass with Bacardi 151 and set on fire. Strain cocktail into martini glass. Like tiny raindrops, drop in a healthy amount of tapioca pearls. Dip cinnamon stick in 151, light on fire without a care and submerge into cocktail. *Now you're starting to see the light!*

CINCINNATI CONNECTION

Each "Spot" can claim their Cincinnati connection in a different way. Original members Jerry Daniels, Charlie Fuqua, Hoppy Jones, and Deek Watson played in different configurations of bands, including the musical comedy trio which played regularly on Cincinnati's radio station WLW, sans Hoppy, called "King, Jack, and Jester." Once they finally all joined forces, they became The Ink Spots, eventually adding Billy Kenny to the group. In 1952, Charlie Fuqua broke off from the group and formed his very own Ink Spots. Legally, he was not allowed to use this name, as he and Billy Kenny both owned 50% of The Ink Spots. Thus he was ordered to use the name Charlie Fuqua's New Ink Spots, but he went against the court and used the title, The Original Ink Spots, which put out several records on the Queen City's King Label.

BIG MAYBELLE

"WHOLE LOTTA SHAKIN' GOIN' ON."

MAY 1, 1924 TO JANUARY 23, 1972

As a child, Mabel Louise Smith sang Gospel music in her hometown of Jackson, Tennessee. Her larger-than-life presence and personality won the hearts of the audience of an amateur talent contest when she was eight, beginning her journey to becoming one of the most revered songstresses of R&B in the 1950's. As she reached her teen years, she became more interested in R&B, and made the musical switch to the non-secular sounds. She has been described as mountainous in stature, with momentous vocal flexibility ranging from a gravely blues belter to a sweet pop balladeer.

In 1936, Mabel began singing professionally with Dave Clark's Memphis Band, as well as touring with the all-female International Sweethearts of Rhythm. Ms. Smith entered the studio for the first time in 1944, recording with Christine Chatman's Orchestra.

However, her first solo recordings were tracked at King Records in Cincinnati, Ohio, in 1947. While at King, she was introduced to Fred Mendelsohn of the Okeh label; by 1952, he had signed her to the label and suggested her name change. Big Maybelle the recording artist and performer was born. Her Okeh signing brought her first hit of "Gabbin' Blues" which reached the #3 slot on Billboard's R&B chart. In 1955, Big Maybelle worked with the then up-and-coming producer Quincy Jones on a single called "Whole Lotta Shakin' Goin' On" two whole years before Jerry Lee Lewis got his hands on the hit.

Big Maybelle's hits kept rolling and in 1956, one of her top selling singles "Candy" was released on Savoy Records. "Candy" also received the Grammy Hall of Fame Award in 1999. The 1950's were an exciting time for Big Maybelle, not only in the studio, but on the stage, where she performed at the Apollo Theater in Harlem and at the Newport Jazz Festival, sharing the stage with Mahalia Jackson and Dinah Washington.

Big Maybelle continued to record into the 70's, but her last big hit, "96 Tears" was released in 1967, which was a cover originally performed by Question Mark and the Mysterians, and ranked #23 in the R&B Charts and #96 on the Pop Charts.

Big Maybelle passed away in Cleveland, Ohio, in 1972. "Last of Big Maybelle" was released after her death just a year later. In 2011, she was inducted into the Blues Hall of Fame.

HITS

"CANDY"   "WHOLE LOTTA SHAKIN' GOING ON"
"96 TEARS"   "GABBIN' BLUES"

Maybelle's Blues

2 oz *Butterfly Pea Tea*
2 oz *New Riff Gin*
¼ oz *Simple Syrup*
½ oz *St. Germain*
Tonic Water
Cotton Candy
Edible Flowers

✻✻✻ In a mixing glass add tea, gin, simple syrup and St. Germain. Time to get that shake on!!! Once fully shook up, strain into a rocks glass over fresh ice. Top with cotton candy and edible flowers! Start sipping, chatting, and gabbin' your night away with your closest friends! *No need to shed a tear with this libation in your hand!*

Cincinnati Connection

Maybelle Louise Smith recorded three singles at Cincinnati's King Records in **1947**, which happened to be her first solo tracks. While in Cincinnati, she was discovered by Fred Mendelson, who gave her the name **Big Maybelle**, and signed her to Okeh records.

MEMPHIS SLIM

SEPTEMBER 3, 1915
TO
FEBRUARY 24, 1988

John "Peter" Chatman was one of the most prolific Blues piano players of all time. Mr. Chatman learned the value of being true to one's craft and inventing his own style to connect to the piano's ivories. His right hand floated around the treble, riffing effortlessly, while the left hand walked strong and steady on the bass. His voice was a hybrid of crooner and blues shouter.

Chatman's father had a group called the Washboard Band which featured Roosevelt Sykes, an influential Blues pianist from whom Chatman found inspiration. Chatman taught himself to play the piano and began touring the loud and boisterous juke joints and dance halls of the south, playing under his father's name.

Those touring experiences prepared him for his move to Chicago where he found himself performing in the company of Big Bill Broonzy and Sonny Boy Williamson. Chatman got a great piece of advice from Broonzy, who told him that he needed to come up with his own style, separate from the sound he emulated from his mentor Sykes. Chatman then began to embody the very soul and energy of the juke joints he played early in his career, combined with the underlying influence of Sykes, to create his own unique brand of Blues. His first of many (over 500) recordings on a plethora of labels was on Okey, and was released under his father's name. However, when he moved to Bluebird Records in 1940, the producer encouraged him to change his recording name to Memphis Slim, referencing the town of his birth. Although he did change his stage name, he also recorded other records under his father's name in his honor.

Memphis Slim continued playing in Broonzy's band for several years as his accompanist, but broke off to form his own band called the House Rockers, after WWII. His band progressed in the new era of Jump Blues, featuring of course piano, but adding in saxophone, bass, and drums. He and his House Rockers recorded some of his most important hits including "Rockin' the House", "Messin Around", "Angel Child" and "Everyday I Have the Blues" which became a Blues standard providing hits for BB King, Elmore James, Eric Clapton, Sarah Vaughan, Ella Fitzgerald, and Jimi Hendrix, to name just a few.

"YOU'VE GOT TO INHERIT THE BLUES."

Slim's sound was continuously evolving and on the forefront of new Blues frontiers, thanks to his fortunate collaborations with musicians such as Howlin' Wolf's once guitar player, Matt "Guitar" Murphy, and bassist Willie Dixon. Even though Memphis Slim was constantly pushing his sound forward, the emerging Rock 'n' Roll craze was in full swing in the United States, pushing straight ahead Blues on the backburner. Seeking a new, responsive and appreciative audience, Memphis Slim and Willie Dixon left America in the 1960's and began performing in Europe to attentive and ultra-respectful crowds without the racial discrimination and lack of consistent work that they were accustomed to at home.

Memphis Slim made his new home in Paris and continued to record and play as Blues royalty until his death in 1988. Memphis Slim was inducted into the Blues Hall of Fame in 1989, and the Memphis Music Hall of Fame in 2015.

SLIM'S HITS

"MOTHER EARTH"

"EVERYDAY I HAVE THE BLUES"

"GOTTA FIND MY BABY"

"STEPPIN' OUT"

"ROCKIN' THE BLUES"

"MESSIN' AROUND"

"HARLEM BOUND"

MEMPHIS SLIM FUN FACT

Memphis Slim's House at 1130 College Street, in Memphis Tennessee, is located across the street from the Stax Museum of American Soul Music. The house has been reimagined as a multifaceted music venue called The Collaboratory providing space for musicians to rehearse, perform, learn, and record inspired music.

CINCINNATI CONNECTION

By the time Slim was performing with his band the House Rockers, they were touring rigorously, making it possible to record without contracts on several independent labels, including King Records of Cincinnati, Ohio. Although Memphis Slim only recorded one session at King, the company purchased the songs he recorded on the Hy-Tone label in 1948, as well as the masters of those recorded while at the Miracle label.

HEY SLIM!

2 oz Jack Daniels
Bloody Mary Mix
Slim Jim or Vegan Jerky

✲✲✲ Combine Jack Daniels and Bloody mix into a mixing glass and shake. Strain over fresh ice into a pint glass. Step all the way out and fill your cocktail with the most outrageous garnishes you can think of, but make sure you rock it with a Slim Jim or Vegan Jerky. *You can mess around with this cocktail every day. It's perfect for an afternoon pick me up.*

LEMON PIPERS

"TURN AROUND, TAK E A LOOK."

The Lemon Pipers have been described as one of the original Bubble Gum Groups boasting only one #1 hit, "Green Tambourine."

"Green Tambourine" was written by a Brill Building songwriting team, Paul Leka and Shelley Pinz as an answer to failed chart toppers written by the band themselves. Their label, Buddah Records, forced them out of their Psychedelic genre into a Bubble Gum Pop band.

The Lemon Pipers records had a kind of duality to them with some of the songs true to their artistic roots, while others written in the Brill Factory. After a few more tries at saccharine sweet songs, they finally gained the artistic control they craved.

They immediately fell off the charts, leading to an ultimate band break up after only three years. You may have heard of original guitar player, Bill Bartlett. He joined the band Ram Jam who recorded a well know rendition of "Black Betty" which was originally reworked by founding members of The Lemon Pipers.

YEARS MOST ACTIVE
1966 TO 1969

HITS

"GREEN TAMBOURINE"

"RICE IS NICE"

Green Tambourine

Absinthe Rinse
1½ oz. Watershed Gin
½ oz. Chartreuse
½ oz. Simple Syrup
½ oz. Lemon Juice
Lemonhead Rim
Bubble Gum
Kiwi Round

✱✱✱ On a small plate, crush three lemonheads with a muddler and set aside. Lightly coat your coupe with absinthe. Set aside. Combine gin, Chartreuse, lemon juice, and simple syrup in a mixing glass. Fill the glass with ice and shake like a tambourine until it's oh so nice. Grab the coupe and run a kiwi round along the rim of the glass then dip into lemon bits. Strain the cocktail into coupe, garnish with kiwi slice, and *you've got a drink you can really chew your bubble gum to.*

Cincinnati Connection

The Lemon Pipers formed in 1966 in Oxford, Ohio, playing regularly in several underground clubs in both Oxford and Cincinnati, including the iconic Ludlow Garage, owned then by popular City Council member Jim Tarbell. The Ludlow Garage hosted concerts from 1969-1971 with world renowned acts, namely The Allman Brothers, Santana, The Kinks, B.B. King and many more. It has since re-opened and is currently Rockin' 'n' Rollin'.

CATHY CARR

JUNE 28, 1936 TO NOVEMBER 22, 1988

"YOU'LL FIND TRUE LOVE HAS ITS CHARMS."

Angelina Helen Catherine Cordovano's talent could not be denied as early as childhood. She began her career in show business by making appearances on the television show The Children's Hour. Outgrowing The Children's Hour, she found her way to entertaining with the USO and established her stage name of Cathy Carr.

Cathy recorded several songs on the Coral label, which were unsuccessful, but led her to a new label, Fraternity Records, based out of Cincinnati, Ohio. It was at Fraternity that she began recording and releasing singles. Her third release, "Ivory Tower," was a big hit charting #2 on the Billboard Pop Chart. Cathy experienced a smaller success on Fraternity with the single "Heart Hideaway" which worked its way up to #67 on the pop charts.

After Fraternity, Carr moved onto Roulette Records where she released a few singles ranging from #63 to #103 on the charts. Cathy wanted to try her hand at more adult, sultry music, yet she found herself back into the teenybopper crowd with her last hit "Sailor Boy." As pop music evolved and Rock 'n' Roll became more prominent on the listeners' turntables, as well as the no-longer-a-teenager Cathy was dancing with adulthood, she recorded her last single on RCA in 1967.

HITS

"IVORY TOWER"

"HEART HIDEAWAY"

"SAILOR BOY"

"FIRST ANNIVERSARY"

"LITTLE SISTER"

"I'M GONNA CHANGE HIM"

Ivory Tower

1 ½ oz Gin
½ oz Kahlua
½ oz Fernet Branca Menta
1 oz Cream
½ oz Vanilla Simple Syrup
Egg White
Soda Water
Mint
Coconut Bonbons

*** Combine gin, Kahlua, Fernet, cream, vanilla syrup, and egg white in a mixing glass and vigorously shake dry (without ice.) Add some ice and shake, shake, and shake your heart out some more. Strain into a milkshake glass and top with soda. Stick a sprig of mint into a tipping tower of coconut bonbons. *No reason to change a thing now!*

Cincinnati Connection

Cathy Carr called Cincinnati's Fraternity Record Label "home" for her first big successes as a recording artist. Her biggest hit, "Ivory Tower," was a Fraternity release bounding all the way to #2 on Billboard's Pop Chart.

OHIO PLAYERS

"GIVE IT TO ME STRAIGHT BABY."

The Ohio Players had a revolving door of band members throughout the years and some of the Players are said to be performing together to this day. The band was known as a party band as well as a house studio group from Dayton, Ohio. The Players were original members of Cleveland State University's R&B Hall of Fame and cut its teeth under the name "Greg Webster and the Ohio Untouchables."

The Ohio Players incorporated an outstanding horn section and flamboyant costumes, always highlighting their astrological signs and throwing in lots of double entendre. Their record covers were more than risqué and pushed all of the buttons on all of the butterfly collared shirts in the 70's. They are known as the "The Ohio Players" to reference both being musicians and their attentiveness to the ladies...wink wink...

YEARS MOST ACTIVE
1959 TO 2002

HITS

"FUNKY WORM"

"FIRE"

"LOVE ROLLERCOASTER"

"JIVE TURKEY"

36 ROCKTAILS: AN AMPED UP SPIN ON MIXOLOGY

Jive Turkey

1½ oz *Wild Turkey Rye*
½ oz *Watershed Nocino Black Walnut Liqueur*
2 *Dashes Cardamom Bitters*
Rhinegeist Dad Holiday Ale
Orange Peel

✱✱✱ Combine rye, Nocino, and bitters in a mixing glass. Fill glass with ice and shake yer tail feather. With love, strain into a large rocks glass. Top with beer until frothy and garnish with a flamed orange peel. *Now it's just hot enough for you to put your lips to!*

Cincinnati Connection

The Ohio Players includes members who have resided and/or are still residing in Cincinnati. Dayton, Ohio is just a hop, skip, and a jump north of Cincinnati, so we like to share bragging rights.

RALPH STANLEY

FEBRUARY 25, 1927 TO JUNE 23, 2016

Dr. Ralph Stanley was awarded an honorary Doctor of Music from Lincoln Memorial University in Harrogate, Tennessee, in 1976; he received a second honorary Doctor of Music degree from Yale University in 2014. This Doctor of Music was the first inductee in the third millennium into the Grand Ole Opry, and won a Grammy for his work on the film "O Brother, Where Art Thou" in 2002. His accomplishments are a long list of awards and recognitions as an international ambassador of Bluegrass music, which continued to queue up all the way to his passing at age 89 in 2016.

Ralph Stanley grew up in southwest Virginia in a tiny town called McClure, where he would occasionally hear his father singing church songs, such as "Man of Constant Sorrow" which became part of his popular repertoire. Dr. Stanley credits his banjo playing to his mother's style of 5-string banjo, and in trying to emulate her claw hammer technique, invented his own way of picking. Stanley's mother had 11 brothers and sisters, all of whom played the banjo, and they would play at "gatherings around the neighborhood, like bean stringin's." He received his first banjo as a gift around the age of 15. His parents owned a general type of store and his aunt sold the instrument to his mom for $5 in which was paid for in groceries from the store.

After his high school graduation, Ralph was inducted into the army, serving a little more than a year. Immediately upon returning home, his father and his brother, Carter, picked him up from the station and drove their way to a radio studio where Carter was scheduled to perform on air with Roy Sykes and the Blue Ridge Mountain Boys. Ralph joined them on vocals, citing that he "sang on the radio before he even got home from the army."

Setting aside a sensible education in veterinary

> "Ralph found it in the music of the mountains, in the hollows, in the people and in the churches."
> — RICKY SKAGGS

school, Ralph decided to join his guitar playing brother to form the Clinch Mountain Boys - a band influenced by the area they grew up in mixing the emerging Bluegrass sound with the Appalachian singing styles of Primitive Baptist Universalist Church. The Church did not believe in Hell; rather, Hell is actually experienced in this earthly life. The Clinch Mountain Boys blended the harmonies of their musical Carter family, playing mainly covers of the Father of Bluegrass, Bill Monroe's music. The brothers eventually realized they needed to write their own songs and create their own sound, thus forming the band The Stanley Brothers and signed with Columbia Records.

In the 1950's, The Stanley Brothers and their band, The Clinch Mountain Boys, signed with King records in Cincinnati and continued to coin the "Stanley Style" of Bluegrass that is most commonly known today. After his brother's passing in 1966, Dr. Ralph Stanley maintained the band name throughout his solo career. To read more about Ralph Stanley in his own truth, please find his autobiography *Man of Constant Sorrow: My Life and Times*.

RALPH'S HITS

"O DEATH"

"I'LL FLY AWAY"

"MAN OF CONSTANT SORROW"

"MOUNTAIN DEW"

"HEMLOCK AND PRIMROSES"

"PRETTY POLLY"

FUN TWISTED KING FACT

"Finger Poppin' Time" was written by Hank Ballard, who also wrote "The Twist." Not only did Hank Ballard record this tune on King, but so did The Stanley Brothers. According to Ralph, James Brown and his band happened to be in the studio while The Stanley Brothers were laying down the tracks and "James and his band were poppin' their fingers on that."

CINCINNATI CONNECTION

The Stanley Brothers and the Clinch Mountain Boys were signed to Cincinnati's King Label. In fact, when Ralph's brother passed, he was unsure if he should or could continue without him. He received "3,000 letters and phone calls" encouraging him to keep going. He talked with Syd Nathan, King's owner, and asked if he wanted to continue his contract without Carter. Syd apparently said, "Hell yes!"

PRETTY POLLY

1½ oz Amaretto
¾ oz Brown Sugar Pecan Simple Syrup
½ oz Lemon Juice
Egg White

✳✳✳ Combine all ingredients and dry shake (shake without ice) hard for 30 seconds in a vigorous style. Shake it so hard that Stanley himself would commend your actions! Add a few cubes of ice and shake until you hear the last cube rattle in the tin. *Strain into a tall coupe and fly away into cocktail bliss, leaving all your worries behind.*

THE JUBALAIRES

"PRAISE THE LORD AND PASS THE AMMUNITION."

YEARS MOST ACTIVE
1936 TO 1950s

The Jubalaires were an American Gospel group from Florida that performed and recorded in the middle of the 20th century. As many of the singing groups of their time, a number of performers have claimed a spot in different incarnations of the group, with equally as many name adaptations. They were a groundbreaking bunch, bringing humor and rich gospel roots to a more mainstream audience through their releases on the African American Centric, Queen Label, and later on King Records, Decca and Capitol.

The group began as The Royal Harmony Singers in the late 1930's and by 1942 had a #10 hit on the R&B Charts titled "Praise the Lord and Pass the Ammunition" in which the lyrics quoted the speech of a naval chaplain who was addressing the attack on Pearl Harbor. Hip Hop historians have traced the origins of rap music all the way back to the vocal stylings of The Jubalaires, stating, "They were a Christian Gospel group that sang and rapped with almost the same cadence as the Sugar Hill Gang."

The Jubalaires primarily sang American Folk and Gospel Spirituals, but within their songs, they incorporated what was called Jubilee style singing, which included rhythmic speaking or singing (what we now consider rap) in their verses.

The Jubalaires were featured in several movies, including *The Ebony Parade*, *The Joint is Jumping*, and *The Duchess of Idaho*. With their regular appearances on CBS Radio in the morning, The Jubalaires had to hire a wailing ambulance to get them to the Apollo on time for their appearance at the Harlem Theater in the evening. Even though every original member of The Jubalaires has since passed, their musical contribution to much of the entertainment industry remains relevant and is still revered to this day.

HITS

"NOAH"

"SOOTHE ME"

"THE PREACHER AND THE BEAR"

"BROTHER BILL"

"GOD ALMIGHTY'S GONNA CUT YOU DOWN"

"A DREAM IS A WISH YOUR HEART MAKES"

Cherries Jubalaires

Grand Marnier Rinse
2 oz Cognac
½ oz Cherry Heering
2 Dashes Mole Bitters
Whipped Cream and Black Cherry

✱✱✱ Combine cognac, Cherry Heering, and bitters in a mixing glass. Fill the glass with ice and stir ingredients well. Rinse a martini glass with Grand Marnier and set it ablaze, *letting the flame calm and soothe your soul*. Strain into the martini glass and top with whipped cream and a black cherry.

Cincinnati Connection

The Jubalaires recorded on both Queen and King labels, helping to add to the King Sound, bringing Gospel, R&B, Country, and Blues to their music.

ROSEMARY CLOONEY

MAY 23, 1928 TO JUNE 29, 2002

"I'M THE ONLY INSTRUMENT THAT'S GOT THE WORDS."

Rosemary and her sister Betty started their singing career together after their parents left them to fend for themselves in small town, Maysville, Kentucky. The teenagers were in dire need of money to keep the utilities on so they entered a singing contest as the Clooney Sisters. They were so wonderful that they landed a regular spot on Cincinnati's WLW, earning $20 each per week.

The Clooney Sisters toured with band leader Tony Pastor until Betty chose to move back home. It was then that Rosemary set out on her own, heading to NYC at age 21 to begin her iconic solo career.

Rosemary had countless hits as she made familiar standards her very own with her unique, low and sultry voice. She was nominated for many Grammys, but never won. Her most famous hit was "Come On a My House" (which she claimed to be her least favorite tune in her repertoire) and her most famous movie was her role in *White Christmas*.

Rosemary continued her career in entertainment by collaborating with such stars as Marlene Dietrich and much later Barry Manilow, as well as starring in her own variety show on NBC called *The Lux Show Starring Rosemary Clooney* which aired for a season on primetime television. Ms. Clooney often teamed up with Bing Crosby on recordings and live performances as they shared a tour together in Ireland, and a 20-minute radio program before the news each weekday on a CBS radio station.

Rosemary knew much love and heartache in her life, even marrying the same man twice. Through it all she survived a severe mental breakdown and the anguish that went along with that; likewise, losing her sister to a brain aneurysm marked her moods, as noted in her 1977 autobiography, *This for Remembrance: the Autobiography of Rosemary Clooney, an Irish-American Singer*. The book was then adapted into a movie, *Rosie: The Rosemary Clooney Story* in 1982.

After Rosemary's passing, many recording artists, including Bette Midler, Barry Manilow, and Debby Boone, have paid homage to her unique style and extensive songbook by recording albums in her honor.

HITS

"HEY THERE"   "TENDERLY"   "SISTERS"

"COME ON A MY HOUSE"   "MAMBO ITALIANO"

"WHITE CHRISTMAS"   "THE SWAY"

THE SWAY

1½ oz *Watershed Bourbon Barrel Gin*
¾ oz *Aperol*
½ oz *Domaine De Canton Ginger Liqueur*
½ oz *Grapefruit Juice*
Soda Water
Dried Grapefruit Float
Rosemary Sprig

✱✱✱ *Combine gin, Aperol, Domaine de Canton, and juice in a mixing glass. Fill with ice. Tenderly shake with classic style and rhythm. Strain into an ice-filled Collins glass for a leisurely occasion. Top with soda and rosemary sprig and share it with your family for the holidays!*

CINCINNATI CONNECTION

Rosemary recorded at Cincinnati's Herzog studios on Race Road as well as performed on WLW, a Cincinnati radio station. You can visit the Rosemary Clooney House, in Augusta, Kentucky, on the banks of the Ohio River, where her personal and professional memorabilia is on display.

FUN *WHITE CHRISTMAS* FACT: Veera Allen who played Rosemary's sister in *White Christmas* is from Norwood, Ohio, a small town just north of Cincinnati.

BOBBY BARE

APRIL 7, 1935 TO PRESENT

HITS
"ALL AMERICAN BOY"
"DETROIT CITY"
"MILLERS CAVE"
"SHAME ON ME"

"THE ALL AMERICAN BOY"

One might say that Robert Joseph Bare, Sr., or better known by his fans, Bobby, had a bare bones boyhood. His family split into pieces, sending one sister to live with his grandparents, and another to be adopted by a family who lived down the street, leaving Bobby alone with his father.

To escape from the hardships of his early life, Bobby's savior was country music. He made do by building his first guitar out of a coffee can, a flat stick, and screen wires for strings. As a teenager in Springfield, Ohio, he put together his first band earning a weekly gig at a local radio station about an hour away from their home. As the band gained popularity, they knew they had to take the next step and venture out west in search of fame and a record deal.

As a sign of the times, the band hitched a ride all the way to California with a gentleman who claimed to know Jimmy Bryant and Speedy West (a pair of respected country musicians who were in Capitol Records session band). All the band had to provide this unlikely gentleman was gas money. The voyage turned out to be a tour of sorts, where the band played for tips and gas money at stops along the way.

Once they arrived on the West Coast, they were happy to find out that their vehicular benefactor did in fact have some country music connections, and the band signed their first deal with Capitol Records. They tried releasing a Buck Owens cover, but when that didn't work, they decided to rebrand as Rockabilly, which also did not sell. After losing much artistic freedom, Bare decided to break free from Capitol and join a smaller label. Bobby stayed in California and began playing clubs and building a name for himself gaining momentum as a solo artist with recordings in the works.

Just as Bare was reaching a high point, he received his draft notice and needed to go back home to Ohio to await his induction. It was in this waiting period that Bobby paired up with Bill Parsons and a producer named Cherokee. Cherokee had money and wanted to invest and break into the music industry, thus paying for studio time and session musicians at King Records in Cincinnati. At the end of their session at King, Bobby began brainstorming a talking Blues tune he called "The All American Boy," and in an effort to not lose his muse, he asked if he could lay down a quick recording of it. Cherokee tried to get a copy of the tape for Bobby, but Syd Nathan (owner of King Records) was revamping much of the recording equipment and suggested he take the tapes to Fraternity where they may be able to make copies.

Fraternity loved the tune so much that they wanted to release that very demo on the Fraternity Label. Cherokee asked Bobby for his blessing, and Bobby agreed to a fee of $500 as long as the song was not released under his name for fear of a breach of contract with another label. The deal was made and the song was released with Bill Parsons as the recording artist. "The All American Boy" was in fact a hit, reaching #2 on the U.S. Billboard Charts, as well as peaking at #22 on the UK singles chart, thus unraveling yet another twisted tale of the recording industry.

Bare collaborated with countless musicians along the way, some more well-known than others, such as Roseanne Cash and Rusty York. Bare also made a record penned by the late great Shel Silverstein featuring Waylon Jennings, Jerry Reed, and Mel Tillis.

To this day Bare is touring and performing in the Grand Ole Opry, a weekly country music stage concert in Nashville, Tennessee, that was founded on November 28th, 1925. It is the longest running radio broadcast in US history. Even if you have to drive 500 miles, you need to make sure you get to enjoy Bobby Bare!

48 ROCKTAILS: AN AMPED UP SPIN ON MIXOLOGY

Tequila Sheila

1 ½ oz El Jimador Tequila
¾ oz Sherry
½ oz Sweet Vermouth
¼ oz Simple Syrup
3 Dashes Angostura Bitters
Apple Slices and Pie

✻✻✻ Combine all ingredients in a mixing glass then shake and strain into short stemmed cocktail glass. Garnish with stack of apple slices on the side, and a spoon full of apple pie. *Shame on you for not sharing the rest of your pie!*

Cincinnati Connection

Bobby Bare recorded at King Records where he laid down the original tracks to "All American Boy." He also released a handful of records on the Fraternity Label, where "All American Boy" was released. Oh, the tangled web the music industry does weave.

MIDNIGHT STAR

"NO PARKING ON THE DANCE FLOOR."

Midnight Star formed as a party band at Kentucky State University in 1976 by the Calloway Brothers of Cincinnati, vocalist Belinda Lipscomb, guitarist/drummer/vocalist Melvin Gentry, bassist Kenneth Gant, multi-instrumentalist Bill Simmons, keyboard player/vocalist Bo Watson, and guitarist/keyboardist Jeff Cooper. Their sound was considered to be a party band, along the lines of Earth, Wind & Fire. They were Funk heavy, mixed with R&B, but with a strong synth sensibility. This combination is what set the band apart from others and earned them several chart topping hits off of "No Parking on the Dance Floor."

Throughout the years, members exited the band, most often with the intention of veering out into solo careers as recording artists, producers, and/or writers. Even though the break-up was never intended to be permanent, the talent that was dispersed into the R&B, Soul, Pop, and Funk genres was quite remarkable.

Along with Midnight Star's own hits, the Calloway duo wrote hits for others such as "Meeting in the Ladies Room" by Klymaxx, and "Contagious" by the Whispers, and were instrumental in the development of Cincinnati's own The Deele with founding members LA Reid (Cincinnati) and Kenny "Babyface" Edmonds (Indianapolis) while still involved with Midnight Star.

Although Midnight Star brought their own hits to the charts through the 1980's and into the 90's, the members separately also brought hits to the charts through famed collaborations with other recording artists. Between the Calloway brothers forming their own band, Calloway, with hits such as, "I Wanna Be Rich," to the brothers writing other hits for Teddy Pendergrass, Natalie Cole, Gladys Knight and the Pips, and Levert, to original member Melvin Gentry writing for and touring with Toni Braxton, the band and the brand remains more than relevant in the industry. Check them out on the dance floor today on one of their many world tours!

YEARS MOST ACTIVE
1976 TO PRESENT

HITS
- "FREAK-A-ZOID"
- "WET MY WHISTLE"
- "NO PARKING ON THE DANCE FLOOR"
- "OPERATOR"
- "DON'T ROCK THE BOAT"
- "SNAKE IN THE GRASS"

Wet My Whistle

1½ oz Finlandia Vodka
½ oz Lemon Juice
2 Dashes Peychaud's Bitters
Sugar Cube
Rosé Sparkling Wine
Star Anise

✱✱✱ In a mixing glass, muddle a sugar cube and lemon juice. Add vodka and fill with ice. Shake like you are the star of the stage and strain into champagne flute. Top with a touch of rosé sparkling wine and drop Peychaud's bitters like it's hot! Garnish with a lemon wheel sliding a star on top and wet your whistle! *Call the captain 'cause you got one freakily fun drink!*

Cincinnati Connection

Midnight Star recorded No Parking on the Dance Floor (which went double platinum) in 1983 at Counterpart Creative Studios in Cincinnati, Ohio.

JIMMY DORSEY

"THE BOY NEXT DOOR."

FEBRUARY 29, 1904 TO JUNE 12, 1957

HITS

"SO RARE"

"I'M GLAD THERE IS YOU"

"AMAPOLA"

"SO MANY TIMES"

"TAILSPIN"

"PENNIES FROM HEAVEN"

This story is a tale of two brothers. Jimmy's journey is entwined in his brother Tommy's and to learn of one is to discover the other.

Jimmy Dorsey was born in Pennsylvania, the son of a coal miner who turned to teaching music. Jimmy and his brother, Tommy, being from a musical family, started their own jazz band in their teenage years, called Dorsey's Novelty Six, also known later as Dorsey's Wild Canaries.

Both Jimmy and Tommy performed with many Big Band greats as freelance and studio musicians who backed famous artists in New York, such as Bing Crosby and the Boswell Sisters. Together the brothers earned their chops on coronet, but Jimmy found his fame with the clarinet and alto saxophone while Tommy branched off to trumpet and trombone.

The Dorsey Brothers introduced "The Dorsey Brothers Orchestra" in 1934 at the Glen Island Casino in New Rochelle, New York, where they combined the traditional Big Band sound of a full orchestra with the rhythms and pop appeal of more current dance tunes, tying together two worlds of music while putting their stamp on the emerging Swing Era sound.

It is said that sibling rivalry, and Tommy's desire to branch out on his own, led the brothers to forming their own bands, leaving Jimmy with their original Dorsey Brothers Orchestra and Tommy with his new orchestra. Although Tommy's records out-sold Jimmy's, especially when he brought on Frank Sinatra as the featured vocalist, both orchestras remained two of the most famed Swing Era Bands of the time. Jimmy incorporated a Latin flavor into his arrangements which were some of his most popular recordings including the Amapola (which hit #1 on the Pop charts and remained in that spot for 10 weeks).

Perhaps it was Jimmy's easy-going style as a band leader that led him to workable partnerships in Hollywood scoring feature films and radio broadcasts, keeping company with the likes of Bing Crosby, Bob Eberly, and Helen O'Connell. A singular accomplishment was appearing in *Ripley's Believe It or Not*, when he performed the famed "Flight of the Bumblebee" in only two breaths; he later performed the same song on the live CBS television show *Swing Session* in an astounding one breath.

With the emergence of Rock 'n' Roll, and the decline of the Swing Era, the Dorsey Brothers joined their orchestras and worked together on the film The Fabulous Dorsey's leading to the partnership continuing with "The Tommy Dorsey Orchestra Featuring Jimmy Dorsey" where they appeared regularly on the *Jackie Gleason Show*, and finally hosting their own television program on CBS called *Stage Show*. When Tommy died unexpectedly in 1956, Jimmy took over his band and recorded the second biggest hit of his career, titled "So Rare", on Fraternity Records in Cincinnati, Ohio, which hit #2 on the pop charts and kept its chart residency for 26 weeks. Jimmy passed away less than a year after his brother in 1957.

AMAPOLA

1½ oz Spiced Rum
½ oz Fernet
¼ oz Pistachio Simple Syrup
1 oz Pineapple Aloe Drink
Pistachio Coconut Rim
Aloe Leaf
Old Fashioned Coconut Candy Rectangle

✳✳✳ Here's another unique libation for you to imbibe! First, crush a few pistachios mixed with coconut flakes over a small plate. Separately, combine rum, Fernet, pistachio simple syrup, and pine-aloe drink over ice and shake until you're dizzy! Pour over ice into a tall wine glass. Underneath a row of tri-colored coconut candles, stick aloe in, touching the side of the glass until it hits the bottom. *Sip and smile!*

CINCINNATI CONNECTION

Jimmy Dorsey's "So Rare" original US pressing was released on Fraternity Records, in Cincinnati, Ohio. "So Rare" had been released many times, but Jimmy's version charted #2 on the Billboard Charts as well as #4 on the R&B Charts. The song became the highest charted song by a Big Band in the new era of Rock 'n' Roll, and Billboard ranked this version of the song at #5 for the entire year of 1957, but without the support and tenacity of Fraternity owner, Harry Carson, nothing may have become of it. Once released on January 5, 1957, Harry Carson called disc jockeys at every radio station in Cincinnati and asked them to support "So Rare" for just two weeks. He said if the song did not hit, he would never ask another favor of them. As a result, Fraternity sold 30,000 copies locally in four weeks.

HANK WILLIAMS

"THE FATHER OF CONTEMPORARY COUNTRY MUSIC."

SEPTEMBER 17, 1923 TO JANUARY 1, 1953

Hiram King "Hank" Williams was born in Mt. Olive, Alabama with the condition known as spina bifida, leaving him in pain his entire life. Hank picked up the guitar at age 8 and began studying popular genres of the time such as Folk and Country, and soaked up all he could from the Blues street musician Rufus Payne, whose influence is etched into many of Hank's tunes.

By age 13, Hank had dropped out of school to further his career, as his songs were already on the radio with his backing band, The Drifting Cowboys. Managed by his supportive mother, Hank was also hosting his own show on the station WSFA.

After his marriage to Audrey Sheppard, the couple visited Nashville to meet with the publisher Fred Rose which led Hank to sign with MGM. In 1947, Hank released his first hit "Move It on Over," beginning a career filled with hit singles. Hank traveled back and forth from Tennessee to Louisiana, writing songs and working on radio shows such as Louisiana Hayride, soaking up the native sounds of each location. Called the "father of contemporary country music", Hank's lyrics dripped with both wit and sadness. He was a vulnerable and transparent songwriter, which allowed the listener to relate to each song by placing themselves smack in the middle of them.

Hank Williams recorded 35 singles that charted on the Top 10 in Billboard's Country and Western Best Sellers, with 11 of those ranked #1. After his iconic hit "Lovesick Blues," which was penned and recorded in Cincinnati's own Herzog studios, Hank joined the Grand Ole Opry, where he wrote several songs without the knowledge of reading or writing music.

Sadly, Hank only lived to be 29 years old, passing due to a heart attack in the backseat of his Cadillac in 1953, right after his song "Jambalaya" hit #1, and on his way to a show in Canton, Ohio.

Despite his short life, he made it into several Halls of Fame, including The Country Music Hall of Fame, The Rock & Roll Hall of Fame, and the Songwriters Hall of Fame.

HITS

"MOVE IT ON OVER"   "HONKY TONKIN'"

"LOVESICK BLUES"   "COLD COLD HEART"

"YOUR CHEATIN' HEART"   "HEY GOOD LOOKIN'"

58 ROCKTAILS: AN AMPED UP SPIN ON MIXOLOGY

Hankelada

Light Beer
1 oz Lime Juice
3 Dashes Worcestershire
2 Dashes Hot Sauce
2 oz Michelada Mix
Grippos Rim

✻✻✻ Pour some crushed Grippos BBQ Chips onto a plate. Using a lime, wet the rim of a tall glass. Dip the rim of the glass in the crushed chips, making sure the whole rim is covered. Set aside. Fill mixing glass "half as much" as the glass will hold with Michelada mix. Add in lime juice, Worcestershire, and hot sauce. Fill mixing glass with ice, shake and strain over fresh ice into serving glass. Top with light beer and a lime wedge garnish. *Hey good lookin', why don't you move it on over and cook up this cold, cold cocktail to cure your lovesick blues.*

Cincinnati Connection

Hank Williams recorded his biggest and arguably most important song of his career, "Lovesick Blues" at Herzog Studios in downtown Cincinnati, Ohio. Over the course of two sessions at Herzog on December 22, 1948 and August 30, 1949 he recorded eight songs including "I'm So Lonesome I Could Cry" and "My Bucket's Gotta Hole in It." Herzog Studios was established before King Records and was in business before Nashville built Music Row. You can visit Herzog Studios today and peruse a wealth of memorabilia of the history of recording within those walls in Cincinnati, Ohio.

SKEETER DAVIS

"I'm childlike in many ways. It seems to me like I've been a rebel all my life, too." - SKEETER DAVIS

DECEMBER 30, 1931 TO SEPTEMBER 19, 2004

Born Mary Francis Pennick, it is said that her grandfather gave her the nickname Skeeter because she would quickly buzz around the room like a mosquito.

Skeeter Davis began performing early as a teenager with partner Betty Jack Davis, as the Davis Sisters. Just as they were becoming popular performing on local radio shows and going on regional tours celebrating the release of their signing and record release on RCA, the Davis Sisters were in a tragic accident just outside of Cincinnati, killing Betty instantly and seriously injuring Skeeter. During Skeeter's recovery, she stayed with Betty Jack's mother, Ollie, in Covington, Kentucky, where it is said Ollie kept Skeeter sedated and coerced her into reviving the Davis Sisters, this time singing with Betty Jack's sister, Georgia. They recorded and toured with less fervor and success than with Betty Jack and disbanded when Skeeter was married. During her self-proclaimed "contrived marriage," she suffered deep depression, and decided to try her hand as a solo artist. Skeeter co-wrote the song "Set Him Free" recorded by RCA and produced by Chet Atkins which earned her a Grammy nomination.

Skeeter was one of the first female country singers to be considered a star in the industry. Many of her songs crossed over genres, furthering her pioneer status. She was nominated for five Grammy awards in her lifetime.

HITS

"END OF THE WORLD"

"LOST TO A GEISHA GIRL"

"SET HIM FREE"

"HOMEBREAKER"

"FUEL TO THE FLAME"

A Manhattan for the End of the World

- 2 Bar Spoons Antica Carpano Sweet Vermouth
- 3 Dashes Angostura
- 2 oz Woodford Bourbon

*** Combine all ingredients in a mixing glass. Fill glass with ice. Stir with a bar spoon for about half a minute. If it were the end of the world, that might seem long, however, you would like for your drink to taste its absolute best, so just continue to stir...then strain with a julep strainer into a martini glass (or rocks glass filled with fresh ice, if you so choose) and garnish with a cherry. *You'll get lost in this cocktail for sure!*

Cincinnati Connection

Skeeter Davis was born in Dry Ridge, Kentucky, but her father took a job in Cincinnati, Ohio. The family moved to Covington to be closer to her father's work, which is where she met her partner Betty Jack Davis. The "sisters" would play on Cincinnati's WCPO for only $14.28 a week and also made regular appearances from a live radio broadcast in Jimmie Skinner's record store in Cincinnati called *The Mid-Morning Jamboree*.

MOUSE & THE TRAPS

"SOMETIMES YOU JUST CAN'T WIN."

Were they early Psychedelic Rock? Were they grandfathers of the New Wave/Punk sound of the 70's? Or were they simply a garage rock band from Texas?

YEARS MOST ACTIVE
1965-1969
&
1983-2012

Mouse and the Traps were a perfect specimen of the sound of the mid-to-late 60's Rock 'n' Roll. They combined Roots Blues, Soul, R&B, Dylanesque electric folk, with pop song structure and lyrics that are, for the most part, the opposite of love songs, all while pushing the envelope with recording techniques, vocal effects, and instrumentations.

Most songs were filled with wordy, thoughtful verses and sometimes cheesy (in a perfect pop way) hooks with driving, infectious bass lines. You will hear organs, sitars, tremolo, distortion, Rhodes Jazz piano solos, harmonious backing vocals, strings, and so many more surprises.

Mouse and the Traps were known for their primal destructive climaxes on stage, stabbing their guitars, stomping their instruments and smashing up the stage.

"Mouse" Ronnie Weiss, on vocals and guitar, and Bugs Henderson, on lead guitar, were the founding members of the band. They formed in 1965 under the guidance of producer Robin Hood Brians and they began creating, trying anything and everything in the studio. They found a little bit of success with their single "Public Execution." "Public Execution" is featured on side one of *Nuggets: Original Artyfacts from the First Psychedelic Era 1965-1968*, an epic compilation of American Psychedelic and Garage Rock singles, written by Lenny Kaye. They toured feverishly until 1970 when they disbanded...thankfully, the band got back together, and were still playing until Bug's untimely death in 2012.

HITS

"PUBLIC EXECUTION"

"BEG BORROW AND STEAL"

"MAID OF SUGAR, MAID OF SPICE"

"SOMETIMES YOU JUST CAN'T WIN"

Maid of Sugar Maid of Spice

1½ oz Old Forester Bourbon
½ oz Chambord
¼ oz Ginger Jalapeño Simple Syrup
Founders' Rubaeus Raspberry Wheat Beer
Slivered Jalapeño
Raspberries
Mint

✱✱✱ Combine bourbon, Chambord, and ginger jalapeno simple syrup in a mixing glass. Fill glass with ice. Shake and strain into stemmed glass. Top with Raspberry Wheat Beer and garnish with fresh raspberries and a mint sprig wrapped by a jalapeno slice. *Your friends will beg you for this one because they know it's a winner!*

Cincinnati Connection

Mouse and the Traps were signed to Cincinnati's own Fraternity Records. They had released a few regional hits with Fraternity, but their major Fraternity hit was "Public Execution" which stretched on its tippy toes to reach Billboard's top 100 Charts, cutting it close at number #121. "Public Execution" sounds so much like early electric Bob Dylan that it could be the evil twin of "Like a Rolling Stone."

BOBBY BYRD

"WITHOUT BOBBY, WHERE WOULD THE FUNK BE?"

AUGUST 15, 1934 TO SEPTEMBER 12, 2007

Bobby Byrd was one of the most important Founders of Funk. Bobby Byrd was born in Georgia to a religious family deeply involved in their church's congregation and pillars of their community. Byrd found himself in the church choir, then joined the Gospel Starlighters, a gospel-singing group who were frowned upon by church elders for singing secular music. They soon moved to South Carolina to form the R&B group called the Avons, thus beginning Bobby Byrd's secular music career.

Here we must note that the story of James Brown begins with Bobby Byrd's story. Bobby Byrd had already established the working vocal group The Flames when he met James Brown. He and his family are credited for helping James Brown gain parole from prison in Georgia in the 50's; subsequently, James Brown asked to be in the band. James Brown began as the drummer, but Byrd soon realized there was no way to contain Mr. Brown to the confines of a drum kit. So Bobby decided that instead of competing with him for lead vocals, he would let JB take the lead. Byrd knew that he needed James in the band, one way or another. So there it is! The Flames became the Famous Flames and the rest is history.

Bobby Byrd and the Famous Flames essentially became James Brown's backing band as they began creating their new sound combining Soul, Gospel, and Jazz into what we now know as Funk. Bobby and James co-wrote several songs (many of which Byrd was never credited for). Bobby would warm up crowds as a solo artist at James Brown and the Famous Flames concerts, then step back as band leader for the Famous Flames during the headline event.

The Famous Flames left James Brown in 1968 due to disputes over money, but in 1970, Byrd was asked to rejoin JB's band. It is said that Bobby hired Bootsy Collins and his brother Catfish Collins on the spot to fill in when existing band members had walked out. After that concert, the new band went straight to the studio to record "Get Up/Sex Machine."

Bobby continued to co-write songs with Brown and reaped the benefits of being part of the JB camp, as James produced singles for his band members as solo artists. Bobby married Vicki Anderson, the "female James Brown" who was one of James's lady singers, and the two started a family together. Byrd finally broke ties with James Brown altogether in 1973, while continuing to record and perform, releasing his last recording in 1994.

Bobby Byrd was eventually admitted into the Rock & Roll Hall of Fame in 2007, posthumously, for his role in the J.B.'s, the second version of James's backing band. He also received the Rhythm and Blues Foundation's "Pioneer Award" in 1998.

HITS

"BABY BABY BABY"   "WE'RE IN LOVE"

"I NEED HELP (I CAN'T DO IT ALONE)"

BABY BABY BABY

1 ½ oz Old Forester Bourbon
½ oz Ancho Reyes Ancho Chile Liqueur
2 Dashes Angostura Bitters
½ oz Grapefruit Juice
2 Drops Honey
Papaya
Habanero Chili Pepper
Edible Flowers

✱✱✱ Alright baby, it's time to combine all ingredients in a mixing glass, adding a chunk of papaya at the end. Muddle, muddle, muddle! Add ice. Shake with tin and pour into a rocks glass filled with fresh ice. For full funk, garnish with some hot, hot habaneros and top with tasty edible flowers. *Don't be afraid to ask for help, cause baby, we might be in love, but we can't do this thing alone.*

CINCINNATI CONNECTION

Bobby Byrd recorded in Cincinnati at King and Federal Records in the Famous Flames and as a solo artist, racking up several singles and hits. When The Famous Flames were signed to The Federal Label, Bobby moved with his band to Cincinnati to record. Without Bobby, where would the Funk be?

SPARKLE MOORE

NOVEMBER 6, 1936 TO PRESENT

"OLD KATS NEVER DIE — THEY JUST KEEP ON PURR-R-IN!"

Born in Omaha, Nebraska, Barbara Morgan's blonde pompadour hairstyle was reminiscent of the Dick Tracy comic book character, Sparkle Plenty, and was how she adorned her stage name. She loved to push the buttons of a male-dominated industry by only wearing pant suits while on stage, all the while donning her blonde bombshell image from the neck up.

Sparkle Moore had a short but mighty career in Rockabilly music as she toured the country and opened for acts such as Gene Vincent and Sammy Davis Jr. Her two-ear professional musical career was cut short due to a pregnancy during a time where women were expected to stay home and start a family. Sparkle never stopped writing and recording DIY style. In true Indie fashion, she has released a new collection of recordings in 2010 called *Sparkle-a-Billy*!

HITS

"TIGER"

"SKULL AND CROSSBONES"

"ROCK-A-BOP"

"KILLER"

ROCK-A-BOP

1½ oz Kentucky Wild New Riff Gin
¾ oz Rose Simple Syrup
¼ oz Dolin Dry Vermouth
3 Dashes Orange Bitters
Rock Candy
Orange Peel

✳ Combine gin, rose simple syrup, vermouth, and bitters in a mixing glass and fill with ice. Smoothly and swiftly stir with mixing spoon. Pour into a short, powerfully-stemmed glass and garnish with an orange peel. To really make it sparkle, add some old fashioned rock candy.

CINCINNATI CONNECTION

Sparkle Moore was signed to Cincinnati's Fraternity Records in 1956 where she recorded her four famed singles.

> "It's Official, Family Approved, One Nation, Under a Groove."
> — BOOTSY COLLINS

BOOTSY COLLINS

OCTOBER 26, 1951 TO PRESENT

William "Earl" Collins, AKA Bootsy, began to originate his funky sound while working in James Brown's Band in the 1970's. Mr. Collins' band, The Pacemakers, became the JB's once they began backing up James Brown. After leaving James Brown's band, Bootsy moved to Detroit and it was there that he met the musician George Clinton in 1972. Bootsy joined Funkadelic, and played on almost all of the Funkadelic recordings and all of the Parliament recordings through the 1980's. Bootsy even had some writing credit on some of those recordings. While touring with George Clinton, Bootsy and his brother Catfish Collins, who had been working together since the JB's, formed Bootsy's Rubber Band. Together they recorded the album *Bootsy Player of the Year*, which reached the top of the R & B Charts and released the #1 single "Bootzilla" on the same chart. Without diving into the wormhole that is P-Funk, we must mention that Bootsy had many alter egos to coincide with Parliament-Funkadelic's space age concept where parts of his character grew more and more into the alter ego that became Bootzilla, "the world's only rhinestone rock-star monster of a doll." From this big bang of funk creation, Bootsy's iconic Space Bass was born. During his time in Parliament Funkadelic, the "Original Funk and Roll Wild Child," continued to make a name for himself in Funk music, earning him a spot in the Rock & Roll Hall of Fame in 1997.

Bootsy has collaborated and continues to collaborate with many musicians along the way. One collaboration of particular interest is his work with Jerry Harrison of the Talking Heads to produce "Five Minutes." This was a dance track which sampled Ronald Reagan's "We Begin Bombing in Five Minutes" speech. "Bonzo Goes to Washington" was the band name for this track crediting Bootsy and Harrison as the writers. Bootsy also was featured on Dee Lite's hit "Groove Is In the Heart" where Bootsy and his Rubber Band played as their backing band. Bootsy made the bassline for the track famous and played it live in concerts; although it was, in fact, a sample on Dee Lite's recording of a Herbie Hancock tune.

Bootsy is certainly not a stranger to the many accolades and awards the industry bestows onto hard-working, well-established musical artists. After his many, many collaborations in any and all genres, ranging from Pop to Hip Hop, Rock to Bluegrass, R&B to Soul, as well as being one of the originators of Funk music, along with the hit records, he has won several MTV Music Video Awards, including a Grammy for Best Music Video.

HITS

"SUPER BAD"   "SEX MACHINE"   "FLASHLIGHT"   "BOOTZILLA"
"ONE NATION UNDER A GROOVE"   "GROOVE IS IN THE HEART"

The Bootzilla Collins

1 ½ oz Mescal
¾ oz Falernum
½ oz Lemon Juice
Two Dashes Tiki Bitters
Soda Water
Lemon Rind

✳ Combine all groovy ingredients except soda water in a mixing glass. Fill with ice. Shake, shake, shake! Strain into a Collins filled with fresh ice. Top with soda water, garnish high with as much sexy lemon and lime flares as you dare and you got yourself the most super bad cocktail in the nation. *Yeah Baby!*

Cincinnati Connection

Bootsy's obvious Cincinnati Connection is that of being a recording artist on King Records in Cincinnati, but his light shines on the Queen City in the most beautiful ways, baby. This Cincinnati native is dedicated to uplifting the world not only through music, but on a local level through his humanitarian efforts. To this day, Bootsy's work spans across organizations such as the Cincinnati USA Music Heritage Foundation, Children's Home of Greater Cincinnati, the Association for the Study of African American Life and History, and countless local schools and non-profit organizations.

THE CASINOS

"KISS ME EACH MORNING FOR A MILLION YEARS."

The Casinos won in the game of staying relevant as a Doo-Wop group well into the late 60's during a time where popular music was moving away from the sounds of the 50's. The group formed in 1959 and became a nine-member doo-wop group playing many Cincinnati clubs. Their hit, "Then You Can Tell me Goodbye," though it was a cover originally written by John D. Loudermilk, was recorded on Fraternity Records and released in 1967 and skyrocketed to #6 in Billboard's top 100 chart. Although The Casinos had just one big hit, they had a few other sizable chart climbers as well, both in the US and the UK. To this day, The Casinos still perform nationwide.

YEARS MOST ACTIVE 1958 TO 1969

HITS

"THEN YOU CAN TELL ME GOODBYE"

"IT'S ALL OVER NOW"

The Classic Casino Cocktail

1½ oz Gin
½ oz Luxardo Maraschino Cherry Liqueur
½ oz Lemon Juice
2 Dashes Orange Bitters
Lemon Twist

✳✳✳ Combine gin, Luxardo, lemon juice, bitters, and shake. But it's not over yet! Strain into a coupe and gracefully float the lemon twist on top as if it were your dance partner gliding across the ballroom. You'll love this classic cocktail for a million years and more!

Cincinnati Connection

Born and raised in Cincinnati, Ohio, and signed on Cincinnati's own Fraternity records, The Casinos truly are a Queen City group. Several of the nine members have stayed and reside in Cincinnati, including the late Thomas Robert "Bob" Armstrong, Jr., who was instrumental in installing the lights on the Roebling Suspension Bridge (among other installations on multiple bridges) in Cincinnati.

VICKI ANDERSON

"TOO TOUGH FOR MR. BIG STUFF."

NOVEMBER 21, 1939 TO PRESENT

Texans are notoriously tough and stand up for what they believe in. Vicki Anderson, AKA Myra Barnes, was no exception. Ms. Anderson's "Message from the Soul Sisters," was and IS a feminist anthem.

It's unbelievable how well this song translates to our current #metoo climate in the late teen years of the 21st century in the USA. Vicki/Myra Barnes recorded under both names singing Soul and Funk music with James Brown and his bands on and off spanning two decades. When one listens to "Message from the Soul Sisters" as well as "Super Good" you will hear the undeniable Bootsy Collins bass lines and her then-husband Bobby Byrd (the original founder of The Famous Flames which was James Brown's first official band) on piano. It was this mixture of talent amidst the rest of the JB's under James' production, a Soul/Funk Movement was born.

According to JB himself, as written in his autobiography, Anderson was the best female singer he ever had. "Mother Popcorn" sometimes still takes a sonic stand with her microphone on stage. Occasionally she joins others in the studio for collaborations as well. Raise your glasses!

HITS

"I WANT TO BE IN THE LAND OF MILK AND HONEY"

"MESSAGE FROM THE SOUL SISTERS"

"SUPER GOOD"

"I'M TOO TOUGH FOR MR. BIG STUFF"

"ANSWER TO MOTHER POPCORN"

Super Good

1½ oz Finlandia Vodka
½ oz Sherry
1½ oz Orange Concentrate
1 Drop Rose Water
½ oz Cream
Dried Orange Wheel
Edible Fresh Flowers

✱✱✱ Combine all ingredients into a mixing glass over ice. With a tin, shake it loud and proud for all the ladies! Strain into a coupe and top with a dried orange wheel surrounded by a land of edible flowers and orange froth.

Cincinnati Connection

Vicki Anderson was James Brown's choice female vocalist in his Revue. She recorded and released singles on King Records and made Cincinnati a temporary home while working with James Brown.

LONNIE MACK

"ARREST ME."

JULY 18, 1941
TO
APRIL 21, 2016

HITS

"WHAM"

"MEMPHIS"

"CINCINNATI JAIL"

"CAMP WASHINGTON CHILI"

How do you get to Carnegie Hall? Quit school in the sixth grade and start playing the guitar!

Legend has it that Lonnie Mack traded his bike for a "Lone Ranger" guitar, and his mother taught him how to play. He then quit school in the sixth grade due to an argument with his teacher. From then on, using a fake ID to get into clubs, he began performing as a solo artist, playing in bands and joining in on session work in studios.

Lonnie ordered his iconic Gibson Flying V because it looked like an arrow; later he realized the serial number was #007, making it the 7th Flying V ever manufactured! The rest is Rock 'n' Roll History. Lonnie's influences ranged from his Country/Bluegrass upbringing, to R&B, Blues, and Jazz, and he used all of these influences while recording sessions at King records, backing artists such as Hank Ballard, James Brown, and Freddy King.

Breaking out on his own, Lonnie Mack recorded a version of Chuck Berry's "Memphis" on Cincinnati's Fraternity Label which jumped up to the Top 5 on Billboard's Pop chart. Mack's single "Wham!" from Fraternity's release of *The Wham of That Memphis Man*, both referenced and celebrated his patented use and mastery of his Flying V's whammy bar.

Lonnie Mack was revered and idolized by many iconic guitar players of all genres. He played on a host of popular tracks your ear would recognize such as The Doors' *Morrison Hotel* album where he is featured on "Roadhouse Blues." *Rolling Stone* magazine called him "A Pioneer of Rock 'n' Roll Guitar Soloing."

Lonnie Mack was inducted into both the Rockabilly Hall of Fame in 2005 and the International Guitar Hall of Fame in 2001. His longtime friend, Stevie Ray Vaughan, was instrumental in his epic album and tour *Strike Like Lightning* which highlighted appearances from a stash of celebrities including Vaughan himself, Ronnie Wood, and Keith Richards. The tour ended at Carnegie Hall.

Cincinnati Jail Old Fashioned

- 2 oz Anejo Tequila
- 2 Bar Spoons Vanilla Syrup
- 3 Dashes Orange Bitters
- Orange Rind
- Guitar Ice Cube

✱✱✱ For a wild trip to the illustrious Carnegie Hall, combine all ingredients in a rocks glass. Do a quick stir gradually adding ice as you stir. If preferred, splash soda on top. Garnish with a flamed orange peel and, *WHAM BAM BOOM, you've got yourself an internationally loved cocktail that you can listen to any track with.*

Cincinnati Connection

Lonnie Mack was born about 30 miles outside of Cincinnati. Lonnie was a session musician at both King and Fraternity Records and played on many records for James Brown, Freddy King and Hank Ballard. He released the album *Attack of the Flying V* that featured three songs that referenced Cincinnati: "Riding the Blinds," "Cincinnati Jail," and "Camp Washington Chili." Cincinnati's own Bootsy Collins called Lonnie his musical idol.

THE DEELE

**YEARS MOST ACTIVE
1981–1993
&
2007–PRESENT**

"EXCUSE ME, HAVE I SEEN YOU SOMEWHERE BEFORE?"

This Cincinnati-based band continues to be kind of a big Deele for many occasions. The original lineup of the band, formed in 1981, included a few giant names in the Pop and R&B worlds: Cincinnati's own Antonio "LA" Reid, Carlos "Satin" Greene, Darnell "Dee" Bristol, Stanley "Stick" Burke, Kevin "Kayo" Roberson, Steve "Tuck" Walters, and Indianapolis native Kenny "Babyface" Edmonds. This group was a gathering of incredible individual talent joined to write and record hit tunes.

Their most famous song, "Two Occasions," was released on their third record, *Eyes of a Stranger*, in 1987 and was the only track on the album to feature Babyface on lead vocals. The song peaked at #10 on Billboard's top 100, #4 on Billboard's R&B, and #21 on Billboard's Adult Contemporary charts.

The Deele's debut record, *Street Beat*, was released in 1983 and produced their first big hit titled "Body Talk." "Body Talk" was produced by Reggie Calloway of Midnight Star and reached #3 on the R&B Charts. The next time you come across Miami Vice on the old boob tube, keep your ears open for "Body Talk." It's featured in the "Brother's Keeper" pilot episode.

This super group's sophomore record *Material Thangz*, was not as well received as their first and third, but has a recognizable song in "Sweet November." Although it wasn't a big hit with The Deele, the R&B group Troop covered it and took the tune all the way to #1!

Now, let's talk about the successes of these band members on a more personal level.

You may have heard of the Island Def Jam Music Group, or maybe Epic Records? How about Arista Records? Oh you have? Well then, you probably know that L.A. Reid was president and CEO of these huge labels. Hey, you know the singing group Boyz II Men's song "End of the Road?" Oh you do? Well thank you L.A. Reid and Babyface for writing that tune. Among other awards and achievements, L.A. Reid is a three time Grammy winner. You may read more about him in his memoir: *Sing to Me: My Story of Making Music, Finding Magic, and Searching for Who's Next*.

Babyface has 11 Grammys and for sure you know most of these songs by heart. To name a few, his own hit "When Can I See You Again" and "I'll Make Love To You," was performed by Boyz II Men, as well as "Exhale" by Whitney Houston. Kenny Edmonds began writing songs at an early age. He was shy and found that he could express himself effectively through song. After high school, Kenny met Bootsy Collins and played with him briefly. It was Bootsy who gave him his "Babyface" nickname. One of his first major songwriting credits was "Slow Jam," a tune he wrote for the group Midnight Star on their album *No Parking on the Dance Floor*.

Along with his 11 Grammys, Babyface has countless nominations for both songwriting and producing, working with Bobby Brown, Paula Abdul, Pebbles, Sheena Easton, Michael Jackson, Madonna, and Eric Clapton.

Together, L.A. Reid and Babyface moved on from The Deele to create LaFace Records with Arista Records in 1989. They worked with Toni Braxton, Outkast, Kenny Lattimore, P!nk, TLC, and Usher, to name only just a few.

Darnell "Dee" Bristol was also credited on Mariah Carey's song "We Belong Together" as a co-writer, as well as Bobby Brown's "Roni" and "Rock Wit Cha."

HITS "SWEET NOVEMBER" "BODY TALK" "TWO OCCASIONS" "SHOOT EM UP MOVIES"

Body Talk

1½ oz Light Rum
½ oz Cappelletti
½ oz Chocolate Rose Simple Syrup
½ oz Orange Juice
2 Dashes Orange Bitters
Orange
Coconut Flakes
Rose Petals
Orange Twist

✻✻✻ Combine rum, Cappelletti, chocolate rose simple syrup, orange juice, and orange bitters. Now shake your body like you want to tell a story. Use an orange slice to rub the rim of the coupe or short stemmed glass with in order to make it easier to coat with coconut flakes. Strain cocktail into glass. Sprinkle the cocktail with coconut flakes and rose petals, garnishing with an orange twist for a moment so sweet you'll be sure to remember it for all occasions.

Cincinnati Connection

Cincinnati can hold all the bragging rights for the origins of the successes of this band and the family ties they hold with popular R&B music. With "Every Little Step You Take," The Deele's stamp has been embedded on the pavement of the industry.

ISLEY BROTHERS

"DO WHAT YOU WANNA DO!"

YEARS MOST ACTIVE
1954 TO PRESENT

With each decade, The Isley Brothers maintained relevance as popular musical artists, weaving in and out of sonic trends, always on their toes, traveling through timelines of instrumental twists and tones of the times. Few bands can say they have passed the test of time when it comes to recording and performing popular music, but The Isley Brothers have always been on the forefront of the next big hit, stationed solidly in Gospel, R&B, Rock 'n' Roll, Funk, Soul, Blues, and even Disco genres.

The brothers were born in Cincinnati, Ohio, to father O'Kelly Isley who was a U.S. Navy vet and vaudeville performer, who encouraged them along in their singing at the church. They started performing in 1954 and eventually landed a spot on the *Ted Mack's Amateur Hour* where they won their first significant competition. Their prize? A watch! This watch would represent the first of many hardworking accomplishments, leading them into the elite world of Grammy winners.

The brothers moved to New York in 1957 to secure their place in music history. They began recording on several small labels and broke out with their hit "Shout," which was inspired by a line from Jackie Wilson's "Lonely Teardrop." The Isley's boasts songs on a plethora of labels including RCA, Atlantic, Septor, and Motown's subsidiary Tamla, which produced "This Old Heart of Mine." In 1964, Jimi Hendrix played a short stint with the Brothers stamping his inimitable style into their sound; when, guitarist Ernie Isley joined the group, he carried forward the Hendrix style.

By 1969, The Isley Brothers established their own label, T-Neck Records based out of Teaneck, New Jersey, releasing their biggest hit "It's Your Thing" which earned them a Grammy for best R&B vocal performance. This marked the first of 50 singles placed on the R&B charts from 1969-1988 alone. Sliding into to the 70's with ease, the Isleys mixed together the smooth R&B vocals with funky bass lines and thumping Disco beats. All the while they incorporated these musical lines with the gritty texture of the emerging Rock 'n' Roll sound, the decade was seductively seeping. The brothers maintained their work ethic and their chameleon-like ability to appease enthusiastic music lovers of many popular genres throughout the 80's and 90's all the way to the present, with their iconic musical collaborations and tributes.

Nearly 40 years later, and a far cry from their first prize of a pocket watch, The Isley Brothers were inducted into the Rock & Roll Hall of Fame by the legendary Little Richard in 1992. The Isley Brothers are currently still doing their thing!

HITS

"SHOUT!"   "THIS OLD HEART OF MINE"   "THAT LADY"

"TWIST AND SHOUT"   "IT'S YOUR THING"

"BETWEEN THE SHEETS"   "LOVE THE ONE YOU'RE WITH"

The Classic Between The Sheets

½ oz Lemon Juice
1 oz Triple Sec
1 oz Cognac
1 oz Light Rum

✳✳✳ In a mixing glass, combine all ingredients and shake well. Strain this old cocktail into a coupe and with your entire heart, garnish with a lemon twist. You'll love to sip this classic liquid fusion a hundred times, and it will always come back to your mind.

Cincinnati Connection

The Isley Brothers were originally from Cincinnati in the Lincoln Heights neighborhood, then settled in Blue Ash as teens before leaving the Queen City in search of musical fame.

KENNY SMITH

"GO FOR YOURSELF."

1938 TO PRESENT

Born in Maysville, Kentucky, in 1938, Kenny Smith is a true rare Soul legend who has resided almost his entire life in Cincinnati, Ohio. After his mother's death when Smith was not even one year old, his family moved to the Cincinnati neighborhood of Walnut Hills. Kenny began his career straight out of high school when his first R & B group, The Enchanters, scored an opening spot for Tiny Bradshaw's Eastern Tour.

The group's next success was recording on the Deluxe label, which was a King Records subsidiary, filling in for R&B group The Charms. The Enchanters competed and won a local televised talent show, where their prize was a wrist watch. Unable to figure out how to split up their prize, they sold the watch, divided the proceeds four ways, and dissolved the band. Kenny Smith's first notable work as a solo artist, "Deep In My Heart," was recorded on Fraternity records.

Kenny Smith is a songwriter at heart. His success as a singer/guitar player is, as he says, "out of necessity." Not being able to pay a vocalist or proper guitar player, Kenny learned how to do both in order to get his songs in the studio and on vinyl. He also co-wrote songs for artists such as The Casinos, Leroy and the Drivers, Soul, Inc., and The Dolphins, to name a few, all of which had his songs hit the Billboard charts.

Kenny Smith is, and always has been, an ambassador of Cincinnati music, making sure he gets his foot in any musical door he deems relevant and abundant. Kenny saw a market in what he described as the "Jesus-Rock Era" and wrote and released "Lord, What's Happening To Your People" with the support of General American Records. General American Records in turn made him their Publishing Director and host of their new TV Show, *Soul Street*. Kenny wrote the theme song and interviewed greats such as Lynn Collins, the Ohio Players, Little Royal, the Detroit Emeralds, Gladys Knight, and James Brown. Smith's solo endeavors range from Soul, Funk and Garage Rock.

HITS

"GO FOR YOURSELF"   "ONE MORE DAY"

"LORD WHAT'S HAPPENING TO YOUR PEOPLE"

"KEEP ON WALKING"   "SKUNKIE"

FoxxxFire

2 oz. Glendronach Scotch
½ oz. Cherry Heering
(or homemade black cherry syrup)
½ oz. Grapefruit Juice
2 Dashes Bittermens Hellfire Habanero Shrub Bitters
Black Cherries
Candied Ginger

✽✽✽ Combine Scotch, Cherry Heering, grapefruit juice, and bitters into a mixing glass. Fill with ice. Shake and shake and shake once mo'. Strain into a rocks glass over ice. Garnish with a black cherry pierced into a candied ginger slice. *Go for yourself! This cocktail was made for you.*

Cincinnati Connection

Collectors of Soul and Funk Vinyl records will know Kenny Smith as a Cincinnati Legend who has recorded at a plethora of Queen City labels and studios. He has remained present in his drive as a diverse songwriter, riding the never ending waves of penning that "Next Big Hit." His roots are deep in Cincinnati music history and he continues to kick out the jams. Kenny Smith was inducted into the Cincinnati Entertainment Awards Hall of Fame in 2006, with a re-release of a compilation of Kenny's most loved tracks.

NINA SIMONE

FEBRUARY 21, 1933
TO
APRIL 21, 2003

Nina Simone died in her sleep on April 21, 2003, at her home in Carry-le-Rout, Bouches-du-Rhone, leaving behind a most remarkable musical legacy, which entranced, captured, empowered, and enlightened the entire world.

Nina's work was unapologetically authentic, and at times necessarily brutally honest, digging deep into political activism, black pride, and feminine power. The High Priestess of Soul's undeniable lyrical ability to perform a popular song on her own terms, in her own truth, through her own arrangements and phrasing, captivates listeners to this day, but Nina Simone did not start out as a vocalist.

Born Eunice Waymon in Tryon, North Carolina, on February 21, 1933, this young lady proved to be a musical prodigy, playing the piano by ear at age 3.

The daughter of a Methodist minister and preacher, Eunice was raised in the church and thusly practiced good morals and manners, learned to carry herself with pride and dignity, and understood the value of hard work. Young Ms. Waymon began playing piano in her mother's church, using her remarkable ability to play anything and everything presented to her by ear. Recognizing her talent, her parents sought out a classical piano teacher to help her learn to read the great classical pieces, and plant deep roots and love of the likes of Bach, Chopin, Beethoven, Schubert, and Brahms, which is ever-present in her popular recordings and musical interpretations as Nina Simone.

Eunice graduated valedictorian of her high school class, and her community raised funds for her to attend Julliard as a concert pianist...but those funds only took her through the summer.

She then applied for the prestigious Curtis Institute of Music in Philadelphia, and in spite of a brilliant audition, was denied acceptance due to racial discrimination. After these educational defeats, Eunice began to teach music to private students and play in the Midtown Bar & Grille in Atlantic city in New Jersey, incorporating Jazz and Blues into her Classical roots, eventually add-

> "...Make people feel on a deep level. It's difficult to describe because it's not something you can analyze; to get near what it's about you have to play it. And when you've caught it, when you've got the audience hooked, you always know because it's like electricity hanging in the air."
> — NINA SIMONE

ing in vocals out of necessity placed on her by the club owners. In order to not shame her family and Church by singing and playing non-secular music, she then changed her name to Nina Simone.

Word spread of her talents, thus beginning her famed musical career born from her adaptations of Gershwin's Porgy and Bess, and other Jazz standards leading to a fervent catalogue of both original and standard tunes spanning any and all genres, from Jazz to Blues, Folk to Rock & Roll, Soul to Musical Theater; no musical stone was left unturned.

In addition to being a blessed interpreter of popular music, Nina Simone found her political voice when she penned "Mississippi Goddamn" opening a new avenue in which she could share her truth and voice. Following the inconsequentially radio-banned "Mississippi Goddamn" was "Four Women" and her haunting version of Billie Holiday's "Strange Fruit," bearing witness to her pointed focus on using her recordings and live performances to promote civil activism.

Nina became friends and collaborators with Harlem poets, playwrights, and authors such as Lorraine Hansberry, James Baldwin, and Langston Hughes. Nina's "Backlash Blues" was inspired by and quoted Langston Hughes' last written poem, which he gave to Nina to turn into a musical piece; and "To Be Young, Gifted and Black" was honoring Lorraine Hansberry, taking the song title from a work in progress play Hansberry had been writing before she passed.

Throughout the 1970s and early 1980s, Nina resided in many countries outside of the US, including Barbados, Liberia, Belgium, England, and France. Nina Simone continued to record and play live, and released her final album in 1993 entitled *A Single Woman in Southern France*. You may read about Nina's life in her autobiography *I Put a Spell on You*, which she penned in 1992.

NINA'S HITS

"I LOVES YOU PORGY"

"LOVE ME OR LEAVE ME"

"FEELIN' GOOD"

"I PUT A SPELL ON YOU"

"BABY JUST CARES FOR ME"

"MISSISSIPPI GODDAMN"

"FOUR WOMEN"

"THE LOOK OF LOVE"

"BACKLASH BLUES"

"DO I MOVE YOU"

"TO BE YOUNG, GIFTED, AND BLACK"

CINCINNATI CONNECTION

Nina Simone had begun a working relationship with Bethlehem Records, a Jazz label based out of New York in 1957. The owner of the label, Gus Wildi, told Nina she could record whichever tunes, however she pleased, with whomever she chose, and she did just that.

Fourteen songs recorded in 14 hours in one session with her handpicked trio. Eleven of these 14 tracks ended up being her *Little Girl Blue* album with titles such as "I Loves You Porgy" and "My Baby Just Cares for You." She had a one-year contract with Bethlehem, which was soon ending, as well as the Bethlehem label itself. Gus couldn't properly fund the distribution of the titles on his label, so he left the recording dormant on a proverbial shelf.

In 1958, Wildi sold half of the label for distribution to Syd Nathan, owner of Cincinnati King Records, giving King exclusivity of worldwide Bethlehem distribution. It is said the minute Nina's contract was to expire with Bethlehem, Syd Nathan showed up on her doorstep with a list of songs that he wanted her to record and list of players with whom she would record them.

Bold and strong, Simone basically sent him away saying that her agreement with Gus was otherwise and she would hold all the artistic reins. Syd Nathan was not used to being met with such a response and in turn, put *Little Girl Blue* on the back burner and didn't release it until after her Bethlehem contract had officially ended. Even once released, he barely put forth any effort saying it was just a "local thing" and not for wide distribution. Fortunately, a radio DJ in Philadelphia fell in love with her Gershwin interpretation of "I Loves You Porgy" and played it incessantly on air until the song became a hit. Word caught on in NYC and eventually the rest of the country taking "Porgy" to the #2 slot on Billboard's R&B charts, and #18 in Billboard's Hot 100 Pop Charts, making it Bethlehem's biggest hit.

Real Real

1 ½ oz Glendronach Scotch
½ oz Benedictine
½ oz Cotes de Rhône (white)
Sugar Cube
2 Dashes Transatlantic Bitters
Dried Lemon Wheel

*** In a mixing glass, muddle a sugar cube with the bitters into a paste. Add the Benedictine and give it a reverent stir. Add in the scotch, wine and ice. Move the mixture around the ice cubes with elegance and grace. Strain into a large snifter and garnish with a dried lemon wheel. This smooth drink feels as good as the look of love. *You won't be lonely with this baby by your side! Does it move you to fall in love with it over and over?*

H-BOMB

"THE COBRA KID"

MAY 9, 1929 TO NOVEMBER 26, 2006

Robert Purcell Ferguson was the 11th of 12 children of a Southern Baptist preacher in South Carolina. At age six, Ferguson began playing piano in his father's storefront Baptist Church. His father agreed to pay for lessons on the premise that he would only learn "sacred melodies."

It didn't take long before Ferguson began to slam out the blues, and by age 19 he went on his lone path to New York City. He jumped on a tour with Joe Liggins and his Honeydrippers. Once established in NYC, Ferguson broke off solo style by securing a solid gig in Harlem at the Baby Grand Club, billed as "The Cobra Kid."

He recorded on his first label, Derby Records, as Bob Ferguson, but as a true "Blues Shouter" he soon earned the name of H-Bomb with his explosive dynamics and witty charm. He was a pioneer of this new Rock 'n' Roll style emerging in the mid-1950's. His full band sound featured driving primal rhythms, walking bass lines, perfectly shouted dirty vocals, effortlessly but intentionally slammed out piano grooves and trills, and sometimes honking tenor saxophone solos.

He recorded extensively in the 1950's for such labels as Derby, Atlas, Savoy, Prestige, Specialty, and Federal and toured with legends such as Redd Foxx, Ruth Brown and Clarence "Gatemouth" Brown, singing and telling jokes. He formed his own band, H-Bomb and his Mad Lads, and developed his own style, with more attention to his piano playing, touring through the 1960's.

After a brief hiatus in the 1970's, H-Bomb realized he couldn't stay away from the sonic sounds that surged through his veins. He suddenly emerged for his comeback unapologetically scratching his itch to perform while donning colorful flamboyant wigs and headdresses, exuding the intensity and soul you feel from his art. He blew into the clubs debuting a new persona with every show. Never would you experience the same wig twice.

H-Bomb returned to the recording studio in 1985 to release two singles on the Radiation label. His comeback brought the house down during the Chicago Blues festival in 1992 where he was backed by his then-new band, The Medicine Men. Together they waxed his first album in 1993, *Wiggin' Out* for Chicago's Earwig label showcasing his wild-as-ever persona. The Medicine Men are still playing consistently today in Cincinnati, Ohio.

HITS

"DOUBLE CROSSIN' DADDY" "YOU MADE ME BABY"

"LIFE IS HARD" "MEATLOAF" "GOOD LOVIN"

The H-Bomb

1 ½ oz Finlandia Vodka
1 oz Amaro Averna
Grapefruit Stiegl Radler
Orange Slices

*** In a mixing glass, combine vodka and Averna. Shake it hard and strain into a tall glass without ice. Top with Radler and garnish with an orange slice or two. Easy enough? *Life can be hard, you deserve a good drink you'll want to call home twice to papa about.*

Cincinnati Connection

H-Bomb moved to Cincinnati in 1957 to sign with King Records. His recording on the King subsidiary Federal Records included "Mary, Little Mary" and "Midnight Ramblin' Tonight." Once he moved to the Queen City, he never wanted to leave.

HANK BALLARD

NOVEMBER 18, 1927 TO MARCH 2, 2003

"HOW YOU GONNA' GET RESPECT (IF YOU HAVEN'T CUT YOUR PROCESS YET)?"

The music business was and always will be a bit "twisted," and Hank's story doesn't stray from the confusing twists and turns of the business we call "show." John Henry Kendricks, AKA Hank Ballard, was at the very heart of R&B and Rock 'n' Roll with his willingness and energy to push the envelope combining sexually explicit lyrics with the rhythms and sounds of Gospel Music.

Ballard's groups had the reputation for being some of the most risqué in the business and were even banned from the radio. When his songs hit, they stayed on the charts for years, and sold millions of copies even after being banned.

The story of "The Twist" is a confusing one as it began with Hank "borrowing" the melody of a Midnighter's tune that never charted, which in turn had actually been "borrowed" from a Drifters tune called "Whatcha Gonna Do." King Records decided to pick up Ballard and "The Twist" was put it on the B side of the Hank's Gospel Ballad "Teardrops on Your Letter."

Here is where it becomes even more of a music business labyrinth: Dick Clark of American Bandstand loved "The Twist" so very much that although it was the first record to actually credit Hank Ballard by name, Clark commissioned Chubby Checker to re-record it. Chubby Checker made the song a chart topper not once, but three times! Hank Ballard was rightfully inducted into the Rock 'n' Roll Hall of Fame in 1990.

HITS

"THE TWIST"

"FINGER POPPIN' TIME"

"WORK WITH ME ANNIE"

"LET'S GO, LET'S GO, LET'S GO"

"ANNIE HAD A BABY"

"GET IT"

"SEXY WAYS"

THE TWIST

2 oz. Byrrh Sweet Vermouth
½ oz. Lemon Juice
Sparkling Wine
Very, Very Long Lemon Twist

✱✱✱ Combine lemon juice and Byrrh in a mixing glass. Fill with ice. Shake and strain into a champagne flute. Top with sparkling wine and garnish with the longest, sexiest, most poppin' twist you can possibly make. Let it spill over onto the dance floor. Get it, got it, LET'S GO!

CINCINNATI CONNECTION

Hank Ballard recorded on both Federal and King labels. After his success with the Midnighters, he went solo and performed in James Brown's revue, where he released minor hits produced by James Brown, "How You Gonna Get Respect (If You Haven't Cut Your Process Yet)" and "From The Love Side."

HARV

"SHAKE YOUR BOOTY AND FEEL THE MUSIC, YOU WILL ALWAYS BE LOVED!"

JUNE 9, 1978 TO NOVEMBER 13, 2018

Angela Harvey, or DJ Harvination as she was known to many Ohioans, lived and breathed music. For 20 years she was a DJ in the greater Cincinnati area. Through music, she created a family of friends and fans that valued her immensely and became her tribe. She was a staple in Cincinnati and touched the lives of everyone she came across. Her presence was intoxicating and you felt loved just being near her. Over the years, she extended her circle of kinship by working with STAR FIRE and fostering many children in need, whom she grew to love as if they were her own. Harv was diagnosed with the thief disease ALS in her late 30's, and lived with it, working hard to kick the disease on its ass, tirelessly and defiantly showing the world that she would not give up the battle with her imminent disease. Shortly after her 40th birthday, Harv put down her boxing gloves, and wound down her turntables. Her spirit and her music still lives on in the hearts of the community and will always be treasured in their memories and beyond.

The Harvination

1 ½ oz Vodka
½ oz Cream
½ oz Kahlua
Birch Beer
Splash of Soda water

*** In a clear mixing glass combine vodka, cream and Kahlua. Grab a mixing tin and with your tin and glass shake your booty like you're dancing the night away. Strain into a pint glass over ice. Top with birch beer to get to the root of the drink. Splash some soda water on top to add a funky froth that will start your night off right. You'll forever give your love to this kind and sweet libation that will touch you soul!

QUICK GUIDELINES
FOR CRAFTING YOUR OWN COCKTAILS

There are a few general rules to crafting a cocktail which we thought we would lightly touch upon before you dive into your bar and start mixing.

THE STARTING POINT IS CHOOSING CORRECTLY WHEN YOU SHOULD *STIR*, AND WHEN YOU SHOULD *SHAKE*.

You will shake a cocktail when using fruit juice, egg whites, or cream. The mixing tin is for shaking! *(See fig. 1)*

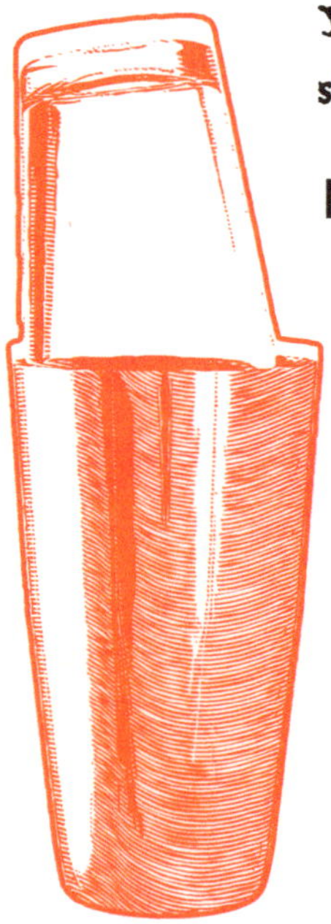

NEXT, WHEN STRAINING A COCKTAIL YOU HAVE SHAKEN, YOU WILL TYPICALLY USE THE HAWTHORN STRAINER, WHICH HAS THE SPRING AT THE TOP. *(See fig. 2)*

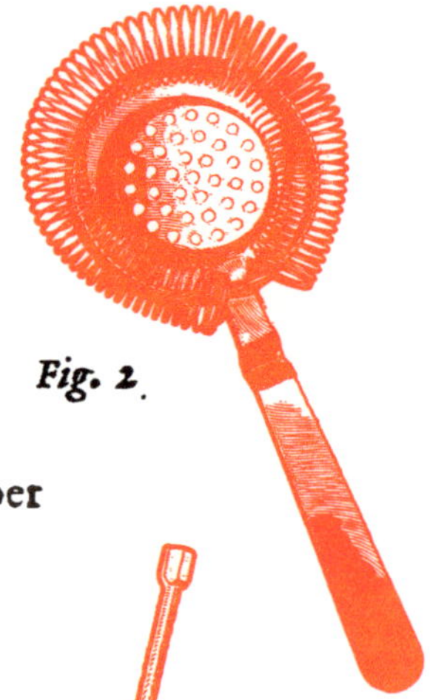

You may also take the spring off for a dry shake on an egg white cocktail and return it to its proper position when straining into the cocktail glass.

YOU WILL STIR A COCKTAIL WHEN THE INGREDIENT LIST IS ALL BOOZE.

For a martini type of drink, you will mainly use the Julep Strainer, which is the stainless round tool with holes in it. *(See fig. 3)*

When mixing your drinks, be sure to add your ingredients into a clear mixing glass (pint glass *See fig. 4*) so you can see your creation.

Fig. 1

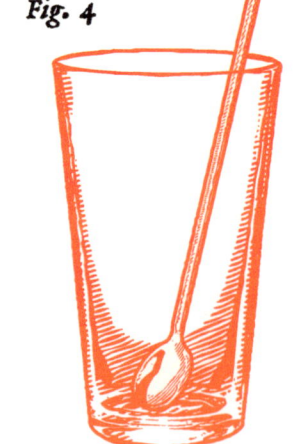

Fig. 2

Fig. 4

Fig. 3

USE HOMEMADE SIMPLE SYRUPS TO ADD FRESHNESS *(See fig. 5)*

We use flavored simple syrups in our recipes, which are super easy to make so you should not at all be intimidated. Feel licensed to explore and get creative with them.

Fig. 5

To make a simple syrup, you bring equal parts sugar and water to a boil in a pot *(See fig. 6)* allowing the sugar to dissolve, then simmer while stirring.

To add a unique flavor, simply add fresh ingredients to the mixture as soon as the sugar dissolves, letting the chosen flavor steep in the syrup while hot.

Remove from heat, let steep for 5 minutes, strain with fine mesh strainer into glass jar, and allow to cool before mixing it into your drink. As long as you keep your syrups air tight, they will last, refrigerated, for about two weeks.

Fig. 6

FRESH ICE IS THE KEY TO A DELICIOUS COCKTAIL

Be sure to always strain your cocktail into the drinking glass with fresh ice if the recipe calls for a drink on the rocks. *(See fig. 7)*

If stirring up an Old Fashioned type of drink you will build the cocktail in your drinking glass, gradually stirring in the ice.

Fig. 7

QUICK GUIDELINES 109

BREWS AND BOOZE
FOUND AROUND TOWN

NEW RIFF DISTILLERY
24 Distillery Way
Newport, KY 41073
www.newriffdistilling.com

WATERSHED DISTILLERY
1145 Chesapeake Avenue
Columbus, OH 43212
www.watersheddistillery.com

MADTREE BREWERY
3301 Madison Road
Cincinnati, OH 45209
www.madtreebrewing.com

FOUNDERS BREWING COMPANY
235 Grandville Avenue SW
Grand Rapids, MI 49503
www.foundersbrewing.com

RHINEGEIST BREWERY
1910 Elm Street
Cincinnati, OH 45202
www.rhinegeist.com

HUDEPOHL-SCHOENLING BREWING CO.
1621 Moore Street
Cincinnati, OH 45202
www.christianmoerlein.com

JACK DANIELS DISTILLERY

280 Lynchburg Hwy
Lynchburg, TN 37352
www.jackdaniels.com

OLD FORESTER DISTILLING CO.

119 W Main Street
Louisville, KY 40202
www.oldforester.com

WOODFORD RESERVE DISTILLERY

7855 McCracken Pike
Versailles, KY 40383
www.woodfordreserve.com

WATERFIELDS LLC
PREMIUM MICROGREENS AND EDIBLE FLOWERS

www.waterfieldsllc.com

AUTHOR BIOGRAPHIES

Kristen Kreft
is a musician, singer, songwriter, teacher of music, dance and theater, as well as a bartender; and most importantly, a single mother. She has an overwhelming desire to create unique, fun, and inspiring tangible and audible works, combining all of her talents and passions. Rocktails is the perfect way to tie it all up in a literary bow.

Mayalou Banatwala
is a singer, songwriter, musician, bartender, and teacher of music, culture, and ukulele; and is driven and inspired to create as much art as possible! She's excited to continue her journey, combing all her interests into this creative venture, Rocktails!

ABOUT ROCKTAILS

Rocktails: An Amped-Up Spin on Mixology is the concept born in a busy cocktail bar in Cincinnati, Ohio, by mixologists and musicians Mayalou Banatwala and Kristen Kreft. While working together side by side for nearly five years, they always had a dream of combining their talents into one really cool cocktail coffee table book. The two had created many cocktails throughout the years, and realized they were often dedicated to musicians, bands, song titles, or lyrics. This shared love of music allowed them to talk to their customers freely about their cocktail creations, and the artists behind the drinks' namesakes. Mayalou and Kristen made it official with a Bourbon "Cheers!" as they now bring you the Rocktails Series.

. . . .

www.ingramcontent.com/pod-product-compliance
Lightning Source LLC
Chambersburg PA
CBHW041947150426

43201CB00004B/43